WHAT IS
Phenomenology?
AND OTHER ESSAYS

James M. Edie, after completing his undergraduate work in this country, spent eight years of study in Europe, at Rome, Paris, and Louvain, where he received his doctorate in Philosophy. He taught at Hobart and William Smith Colleges before becoming a member of the Department of Philosophy at Northwestern University.

WHAT IS

Phenomenology?

AND OTHER ESSAYS

by PIERRE THÉVENAZ

Edited with an Introduction by JAMES M. EDIE
Northwestern University
Preface by JOHN WILD
Translated by JAMES M. EDIE
CHARLES COURTNEY
PAUL BROCKELMAN

 A QUADRANGLE PAPERBACK ORIGINAL
Quadrangle Books / Chicago

Fourth Printing

Designed by David Miller
Manufactured in the United States of America

ACKNOWLEDGEMENTS

I WISH TO THANK Professor Edouard Mauris and the editors of the *Revue de Théologie et de Philosophie* (Lausanne) for permission to translate and publish the articles by Pierre Thévenaz entitled "Qu'est-ce que la phénoménologie" which appeared in their review in 1952 (pp. 7–30, 126–140, 294–316). I also wish to thank the Editions de la Baconnière (Boudry-Neuchâtel) for permission to translate and publish the following articles from Pierre Thévenaz, *L'homme et sa raison,* Volume I: "Réflexion et conscience de soi," pp. 103–121, "La question du point de départ radical chez Descartes et Husserl," pp. 147–165, and "Le dépassement de la métaphysique," pp. 207–237. I wish to thank Messrs. Charles Courtney and Paul Brockelman for their assistance on the translation and Mr. Courtney for his work on the bibliography. Finally, I wish to thank my colleagues, Professors John Wild and William Earle, for reading the manuscript and making several important suggestions.

J. M. E.

PREFACE

PHENOMENOLOGY ORIGINATED with the profound and creative criticism of British Empiricism that was inaugurated by Brentano and Husserl at the very end of the nineteenth century. Many thinkers, coming from different backgrounds and traditions, participated in this criticism, and among them the American thinker and philosopher, William James, played an especially important role. Husserl himself, for example, was deeply influenced by several suggestions he found in James' important and original work on psychology. The result of this co-operative endeavor was the founding of a new approach to the phenomena of our lived existence, in James' words a really *radical empiricism*. This new empiricism has already shown that what was called "immediate experience" and presupposed as the starting point for all conceptual philosophy is not a mere succession of disparate impressions received within a "subjective" mind-container, but rather a vast world of wide-ranging scope with distinctive structures of its own which, for their clarification, require methods quite different from those of the objective sciences. Husserl called this moving historical field of our lived existence the *Lebenswelt* (life-world) and inaugurated the disciplined exploration of this life-world, its essential structures, and its manifestations.

At the present time this disciplined exploration of the life-world is still just beginning. But already enough has

7

been done to show that there is a vast range of facts and patterns to which objective science has no access but which are open to the new philosophical discipline of phenomenology. Some important results, verified by different investigators, have been attained concerning the oriented space of the life-world, lived time and human historicity, the human body as it is lived (*corps vécu*), and a human freedom of world constitution far deeper and broader than what has been traditionally called "freedom of the will." In Western Europe these results have already exerted a significant influence on such disciplines as history, anthropology, and sociology, and in both Europe and America on psychiatry and clinical psychology. In philosophy it has led to a radically novel way of understanding man, and a new approach to what is called philosophical anthropology, which has now been expressed in such suggestive and well-known formulations as Heidegger's *Sein und Zeit*, Sartre's *L'Être et le néant*, and Merleau-Ponty's *Phénoménologie de la perception*. These investigations have also stirred up new approaches and new speculations in the traditional fields of ethics, metaphysics, and the philosophy of religion. In fact, one can only refer to this contemporary phenomenological movement as a renewal of vigorous and disciplined thinking in every field of philosophy.

It is, therefore, of great importance to make the more significant works of recent European phenomenology accessible to the English-speaking world where, since the time of James, investigations of this kind have lagged.

Pierre Thévenaz was a young French-Swiss phenomenologist who taught at the University of Lausanne and who died a few years ago at the age of forty-two. Since that time his stimulating and widely read essays on phenomenological themes have been gathered together, edited by his friend, Paul Ricoeur, and published in a two-volume work entitled *L'homme et sa raison*. Three of the essays translated in this volume have been taken from this collection. In them the English reader will find many suggestive ideas concerning the theory of consciousness, anthropology, and metaphysics which have been developed by an original mind from the fertile ground of recent phenomenology.

All of these essays, and especially the first, will give the reader a living sense of what phenomenology means in our time to an eminent, practicing phenomenologist—its origins in the thought of Husserl, its later development in the thought of contemporary French philosophers, and its prospects for the future. Indeed, I cannot think of any brief introduction to phenomenology that is as accurate and as well informed as the content of this small volume. The translators, the editor, and the publishers have made a genuine contribution to living philosophy by making it available to American and English readers.

JOHN WILD
Northwestern University

CONTENTS

INTRODUCTION

DESPITE THE FACT that phenomenology has been a
living current of thought in philosophy for over
fifty years, there are not more than a handful of
books in the English language which treat of phenomenology in a unified and coherent manner. And even among
those which exist, there is hardly one which offers a serious
introduction to phenomenology as a whole on an introductory level.[1] The following essays by Pierre Thévenaz[2] are
offered as a preliminary attempt to fill this grave lacuna.
These essays are meant to provide the student of philosophy with an introduction of high philosophical merit to
the phenomenological movement as a whole.

For those, and there are many, who have asked for a
relatively straightforward and yet authentic answer to their
question "What is Phenomenology?" Pierre Thévenaz
gives in these pages an introductory answer. The merits of
Thévenaz as a commentator on phenomenology are many.[3]
First of all, as a philosopher intimately acquainted with
and profoundly influenced by phenomenology in all its
aspects, Pierre Thévenaz remained throughout his life
somewhat outside the phenomenological movement. For
this reason he was able to view the movement as a whole,
globally, without personal involvement in the success or
failure of any particular branch of this very prolific school
of thought. His introduction to phenomenology thus has
the enormous merit of tracing the main line of develop-

13

ment from Husserl through Heidegger and Sartre to Merleau-Ponty without ever losing track of its essential unity.
Himself an original and powerful thinker, he is able to discern and delineate the progress of the phenomenological
method as it has developed during these past fifty years on
the continent of Europe. Finally, as an historian of philosophy, he is fully alive to the importance of phenomenology
as a renewal of the principal themes of the Western philosophical tradition, and as one of the most living currents
of thought in the twentieth century.

This selection of essays from Pierre Thévenaz serves the
double purpose of an introduction to phenomenology and,
in the later essays, an introduction to his own thought,
hitherto inaccessible to English readers.[4] Thévenaz died
before he was able to do more than begin his life's work,
the task of writing a "Protestant philosophy." He did not
conceive this project in a partisan spirit, another "re-
gional" philosophy, but as a metaphysics of human freedom, as a study of the human spirit on "this side" of the
divine, striving ever to surpass itself in its continually renewed effort to become gradually human. He did not conceive the task of philosophy to be an effort of escaping from
this world towards the beyond (*versus Deum*) but as an effort of progressively actualizing human consciousness this
side of the beyond (*coram Deo*). In this way Thévenaz remained a "Protestant" without ever leaving the twentieth
century. He placed himself squarely within the French tradition of "reflexive analysis" and, as we should expect,
found his point of departure in the autonomy and spontaneity of the *cogito,* in the immediacy of subjective consciousness, in man's restless effort to discover the "foundation" of his own independence and dignity. Thévenaz
inscribes himself willingly in the tradition of Descartes,

Maine de Biran, Bergson, Lavelle, Decoster, and Lequier, and recognizes as his distant cousins Plotinus and Saint Augustine. Like a Plotinus of the twentieth century, he wanted to renew the Western attempt to establish a metaphysics of consciousness, to analyze and grasp the essence of rationality, its élan and its "consistency." For him, the ultimate metaphysical question concerned the mysterious coincidence of man with himself in the act of self-consciousness; it is this that defines man as man and makes him human.

From such a viewpoint the history of Western philosophy, and particularly the history of metaphysics, can never be simply the record of human errors or a spectacle of mankind's successive mistakes in formal logic. When philosophy ceases to be looked upon as the storehouse of inadequate answers to man's eternal questions, and becomes instead the human enterprise of "questioning beyond questioning," we find ourselves in the presence of an historical and "de-absolutized" consciousness.[5] And it is here that Thévenaz joins phenomenology. Philosophy is not the science of "the eternal"—not even the science of eternally and necessarily valid formal reasoning which is the form that the "Greek ideal" takes today—but rather the progressively achieved awareness of what it means to be conscious (i.e. free, responsible, historical).

These essays have been chosen from the writings of Thévenaz because of their relevance for the history of phenomenology. Only the last two go somewhat further afield and, while remaining central for his understanding of phenomenology, take us a little way into his own specific philosophical position. For our purposes here it is sufficient to point out the originality and tenor of his own philosophical reflexion. We can now content ourselves with examining his view of phenomenology and its situation in the history of man's attempt to understand himself and his world.

As an historian of philosophy, the first task of Thévenaz is to situate phenomenology in the history of Western philosophy. This is, indeed, a difficult thing to do, and we are reminded of the fateful list of antinomies with which Merleau-Ponty opens his *Phenomenology of Perception.* "What is phenomenology? It may seem strange that half a century after the appearance of Husserl's first works we still have to ask this question. Yet it is far from being answered."[6] But the embarrassment felt by a Thévenaz or a Merleau-Ponty in attempting to define phenomenology in a simple, univocal formula is nothing compared with our own. Though the division that separates British and continental philosophy goes back at least to the seventeenth century (it would not be difficult to trace it back to the thirteenth), it has never been more complete than it is today.[7]

Particularly since the Second World War the English Channel seems to have become an impassable barrier. On the continent the appearance of Husserl's *Ideas* is generally regarded as marking *the* turning point in twentieth century philosophy,[8] and whatever their differences, European philosophers speak the language of phenomenology. While in England and America, fifty years later, phenomenology "continues to be an exotic."[9] The result is that, while there exist two major living, vital, expanding movements in philosophy today, both of them interested in the phenomenon of communication, and one of them expressly centered on the analysis of language, they cannot understand one another.

There does not seem to be a single author, at least in this country, who has confronted the deep fissure which divides continental European philosophy from British-

American philosophy at the present time who has not deplored this state of affairs and called for mutual efforts at increased understanding.[10] And this is a significant element in the picture. Those writers who most readily deplore this breakdown in communication and the consequent separation of philosophy into two worlds are seldom the British or the continentals themselves. British philosophers have nearly unanimously washed their hands of continental thought as simply impossible, at best some kind of metaphysical poetry, at worst pure nonsense.[11] The continental philosophers repay this tribute by dismissing the entire enterprise of analytical philosophy (which, after all, like Logical Positivism, owes *something* to Vienna) as trivial, philistine, and infra-philosophical. But American philosophers, and Americans in general, have many lines to the European continent which do not pass through Britain.[12] It is possible that these cultural and intellectual ties give American philosophers an uneasy conscience over dismissing the entire philosophical production of contemporary Germany and France without investigation. Even if we are required to admit, which seems doubtful, that the philosophical differences between England and the continent are due to temperamental differences and even mental characteristics that precondition philosophical reflexion, it can certainly be questioned whether this applies to philosophical thought in America. It remains problematic, but it may be that somewhere in the fertile soil of American thought there lies the latent possibility of achieving some sort of synthesis of the best elements of European and British thought—a synthesis which neither of these silent and monadic philosophical universes will attempt of itself.

Be that as it may, Edmund Husserl's challenge to make philosophy a "rigorous science" is there, and the effort to understand, to clarify, and to develop his method has only begun. Perhaps this ideal of a "rigorous science" of philosophy is one of our chief embarrassments.[13] After Descartes, after Kant, after Positivism, philosophers have renounced such grand schemes. On this continental and British philosophy are at one. Whatever philosophy may be, it is not science. But what did Husserl mean? We must remember that Husserl, too, was from Vienna. The meaning of science, the foundations of science—these are questions which have always interested Vienna (in this Brentano, Husserl, Schlick, Carnap, and even the early Wittgenstein have a common origin). But, for Husserl "the crisis of science" meant the unclarified status of science and scientific knowledge. An unclarified science is a science unaware of its own ontological and epistemic foundations, of its *meaning*. If phenomenology has appeared to many to be antiscientific, it is because they have confused the metaphysics of naturalism with science. What phenomenology does is to "situate" science (as it does any other derived construction of human thought) and to go beyond it in the direction of its experiential roots, its foundations which are to be found in a more original noetic contact with the real. Husserl showed that the world of science was not "the" world it has claimed to be, but a derived construction, an abstraction several stages removed from the primary world of lived experience.

Philosophy is a *rigorous* science for Husserl in the sense that it is an investigation of the most radical, fundamental, primitive, original evidences of conscious experience; it goes beneath the constructions of science and common sense towards their foundations in experience. It studies what all the particular sciences take for granted and what we in "natural" everyday experience take for granted. A "presuppositionless" philosophy is one which will reach what is absolutely primary or most fundamental in experience.

It is in this sense that Husserl establishes the basis for a new kind of philosophy, beyond traditional empiricism and idealism. In his earlier writings he called it a "genuine positivism"[14] and even a "genuine realism,"[15] a "return to the things themselves," a return to experience. The phenomenological method is a descriptive method; the type of philosophy it inaugurates can be called a *radical empiricism*.[16] It cannot be called an empiricism pure and simple, because traditional empiricism from Locke to Russell has been vitiated by its unfounded and unclarified metaphysical presuppositions: its latent body-mind dualism, its empty-mind ("container") theory of consciousness, its conception of the subject as the passive receptor of discrete, simple, atomic impressions from the "outside world," etc. Empiricism has been the least empirical of philosophies because of its metaphysical assumption that philosophy is a science of objects, of beings, and that the subject of experience is itself nothing but another object among objects. This kind of empiricism easily degenerates into a simple and uncritical "scientific" naturalism. At the same time, Husserl's method does not, or at least should not, lead to a simple idealism. It is only by confusing all transcendentalism with subjectivistic idealism that this charge can be brought against Husserl. Phenomenology is neither a science of objects nor a science of the subject; it is a science of *experience*. It does not concentrate exclusively on either the objects of experience or on the subject of experience, but on the point of contact where being and consciousness meet. It is, therefore, a study of consciousness *as intentional,* as directed towards objects, as living in an intentionally constituted world. The subject (noesis) and the object (noema) are studied in their strict correlativity on each level of experience (perception, imagination, categorial thought, etc.). Such a study is *transcendental* in the sense that it aims at disclosing the structures of consciousness as consciousness, of experience as experience; it means to unveil the noetic-noematic structures which constitute the mysterious subject-object relationship which we call *consciousness of . . .*[17] In short, phenomenology is a study of *phenomena*. As such it is a more fundamental study than logic or psychology; it goes to the fundamental structures of conscious experience which constitute the very conditions of the possibility of any conscious experience whatsoever.

However, before we can proceed further, it is necessary to say a word about Husserl's relation to Descartes, particularly because it looms so large in Thévenaz' essays on phenomenology. It has frequently been noted that philosophers can be grouped into two opposing camps on the basis of their attitude towards Hume. In fact, about the only thing which identifies the group of philosophers who practice the logical analysis of language as a school (from Carnap to Wittgenstein to contemporary Oxfordians) is their common veneration for Hume. Can the same place be given to Descartes in continental philosophy? Certainly it is striking that, while Descartes has had such a bad press in England and America, such diverse thinkers as Kierkegaard,[18] Brentano,[19] Husserl,[20] and Sartre (not to mention the school of reflexive analysis which Thévenaz represents) have recognized Descartes as their forerunner in one sense or another. We must, of course, distinguish the early Descartes in search of a method, the discoverer of apodictic subjectivity, from the Descartes who attempted to "mathematicize" philosophy and who elaborated a dualistic metaphysics. It is the *intentions* of Descartes which were pure, not his results.

There are, says Thévenaz, moments in the philosophical evolution of Western man when whole blocks of past philosophy are suddenly rendered obsolete at one blow, and such a blow was dealt to the "objective" philosophies of Greece and the Middle Ages by René Descartes. The merit of Descartes is to have discovered subjectivity as the apodictic foundation for the elaboration of a philosophy of experience. His method of "radical doubt" is the predecessor of the phenomenological method. The recognition of the originality of Descartes and particularly of his effort to establish a metaphysics of experience on a solid foundation, does not, of course, commit phenomenology to the Cartesian metaphysics. In fact, the most solid "metaphysical" point of agreement between contemporary linguistic analysts and phenomenologists is their joint rejection of any body-mind dualism and their concentration on the unitary character of man's behavior as an active, unified, organism in the world.[21] Descartes the phenomenologist and methodologist was far in advance of Descartes the mathematicizing metaphysician.[22]

It is not possible, in this brief introduction, to discuss in detail the problem that, in Thévenaz' presentation of Husserl and Descartes, seems to divide phenomenologists from the school of reflexive analysis. It is sufficient to note that Thévenaz himself does not really believe this opposition to be irreducible. He grants to Husserl and phenomenology the fact that the primary structure of consciousness is intentionality. He reproaches Husserl with not sufficiently recognizing that the intentionality of consciousness does not exclude but rather requires the absolute and empirical (in the sense of "experienced") coincidence of self with self which is the very definition of self-consciousness.

Since the solution of this problem involves the whole question of "transcendental consciousness" and its meaning in phenomenology, we cannot deal with it here in detail. But it would seem that the solution to this difficulty is already implicit in Husserl (at least in the later Husserl) and that Heidegger and Sartre have solved it correctly by focusing more carefully on the "concomitant" or "pre-reflexive" consciousness (of) self which accompanies and conditions any fully-conscious act. It cannot be denied that Husserl up to his final period restricted himself to the analysis of fully reflexive consciousness, to the *cogito* in the Cartesian and Kantian sense. Like all previous philosophers he neglected the pre-conceptual, pre-reflexive substructures of consciousness. It is only with Heidegger and Sartre that attention is somewhat deflected from the fully-reflexive to the pre-reflexive structures of consciousness, precisely because it is no longer "pure" consciousness but *experience of the world* which is the subject of their analysis. We will return to this "enlargement" of the Husserlian problematic shortly. As Thévenaz has observed, this enlargement of the notion of consciousness and intentionality was inevitable once Husserl had discovered the *Lebenswelt*.

Here it is necessary only to distinguish Husserlian transcendentalism from Kantian transcendentalism, a distinction of which Husserl himself became only gradually aware —which accounts for the "idealistic" flavor of some of the formulations of his philosophy during his "middle period" when he called phenomenology a "transcendental idealism." But the "transcendentalism" of phenomenology is not the "transcendentalism" of Kant, though their fundamental *intention* (their motive force) is very similar. The ultimate "transcendental" in Husserl's phenomenology is the *Lebenswelt*, the Life-World as the correlate of constituting consciousness. Kant limited himself to the analysis of the *formal* structures of consciousness, particularly to the transcendental a priori categories of sensation and judgment. For Kant the transcendental categories of judgment constitute the a priori condition of the possibility of any *scientific* judgment. The transcendental Ego is a *judging* consciousness. The accent is on the character of necessity and universally objective validity of fully reflexive acts of judging. On the contrary, Husserl, like Descartes, poses a question of fact,[23] and from this point of view the similarity between Husserl and Descartes is more profound than Thévenaz will admit. *But* Husserl, more than Descartes and more than Kant, is aware of time, historicity, and the intersubjective constitution of life-worlds. Husserl's "Ego" is not the "res cogitans" of Descartes or the disembodied "thinker" of Kantian transcendentalism; it is inserted and involved in the dense world of human life; it is, in his own terms, "life-experiencing-the-world" (*Welterfahren-desleben*).

The fact of the matter is that Husserl is neither Cartesian nor Kantian; he is Husserlian. While Husserl, like Kant, searches for the transcendental structures of subjectivity, it is on the basis of the experiencing ego and its correlative life-world that he does so. He does not content himself with establishing the theoretical possibility of fully reflexive scientific judgments. Husserlian research does not exclude or stop short of the structures of the *Mitwelt* (the world of interpersonal experience) and the *Eigenwelt* (the world of private experience). Husserl ultimately reaches the historical and intersubjective constitution of the *Lebenswelt* and its various modes.

However, it is necessary to admit that, at least in the works published during his lifetime, Husserl does not seem to have fully realized the necessity of distinguishing more clearly reflexive from pre-reflexive consciousness. In the terminology of Sartre it is the *reflecting* consciousness that is the *absolute source,* and the *reflecting* consciousness is never fully *reflected.* It is always ahead of itself, in the world, ek-static, self-transcendent. The lack of this distinction in Husserl's early theory of consciousness leaves him open to Thévenaz' criticism that his notion of intentional consciousness involves an "infinite regress." Let us try to be clear. Thévenaz seems to hold that any rigorously intentional notion of consciousness necessarily involves an infinite regress simply because it is primarily directed towards objects and only secondarily (by a second act) towards its consciousness of objects. But such a conclusion is avoided as soon as it is realized that consciousness is not composed of "parts," that it is not an "optical" phenomenon but an *action.* It is the same consciousness which is *reflecting* and which is *reflected,* and it is because it is *reflecting* that it can become aware of *itself,* reflexively, in the very act of reflexion.[24] Thus in the primary *reflecting* (not-yet-reflected) consciousness we reach an absolute consciousness as the source of all reflexive and thematic awareness. In Sartrian terminology fully reflexive consciousness is necessarily accompanied by a pre-reflexive, non-positional consciousness (of) self and it is precisely for this reason that consciousness can become fully aware of itself. Consciousness, in short, *is* self-relational, self-identical, self-coincidental, punctual, immediate consciousness (of) itself.

To the extent that Thévenaz' criticism of Husserl is justified, to the extent that Husserl did not reach an absolute, factual consciousness, we can say that the contributions of his successors, particularly those of Heidegger, Sartre, and Merleau-Ponty, were necessary for the development of a valid phenomenological theory of consciousness, and hence for the establishment of a viable phenomenological method, as description of *life-experiencing-the-world*.

And this is what happened, as Thévenaz rightly points out, even before the death of Husserl. Heidegger, and later on Merleau-Ponty, extended the problematic of phenomenology in the direction of an existential transcendentalism. Here we must make the very simple Heideggerian distinction between existenti*el* and existenti*al*, between ontic and ontological. This distinction is frequently made and frequently misunderstood. Heidegger is not an "existentialist" pure and simple. While his debt to Kierkegaard and existentialist thought in general is enormous, his basic problematic is very Husserlian. Heidegger's *Sein und Zeit* is an ontological rather than an ontic research. When he examines such ontic and existen*tiel* phenomena as "death," "care," "anxiety," "guilt," "debt," "freedom," etc., he is not examining them in a psychologistic way. Phenomenology is not an introspective psychology. It is not the empirical phenomenon as such that is the goal of his inquiry. He is not simply writing the drama of human pathos and anxiety in the age of technocracy. If this were all we could find in Heidegger, we could easily dismiss him, for others have done better. But he is searching for something more fundamental; Heidegger begins where Dostoevsky, Nietzsche, Kierkegaard, Malraux, and Camus end. The empirical (ontic) phenomena of "death," "anxiety," etc. interest Heidegger only insofar as they reveal the ontological structures of the *Dasein*, of human experience. Heidegger is a transcendentalist and his philosophy is, before all else, a metaphysics of experience. In *Sein und Zeit* he maps out a program for the investigation of the transcendental categories of life-in-the-world. These categories he calls "existenti*als*."

What is an existential category? It is not a category of objects (like the ten categories of Aristotelianism). It is not, at least at first, a category of Being (like the five transcendentals of the Scholastics). Finally, it is not a category of the mind, of the fully-reflexive thinking, scientifically judging subject (like the twelve transcendental categories of judgment in Kant). An existential category is a structure of existence, of experience of the world. Heidegger turns his attention to the pre-predicative, pre-conceptual relationships of the *Dasein* to the world which are the source or the conditions of the possibility of any *experience* of the world. Kant was perfectly right in focusing attention on the a priori categories of subjectivity. But, according to Heidegger, his notion of *subjectivity* was both too "idealistic" and too narrow. He limited himself, first of all, to the categories of fully-reflexive understanding; secondly, he turned exclusively to the subject as *detached from* and *prior to* experience, whereas subject and object arise only *in experience*. The importance of Heidegger's contribution to philosophy and especially to phenomenology lies in his notion of experience-of-the-world (*in-der-Welt-sein*). It is no longer merely consciousness which is intentional (as for Husserl) but the *Dasein,* human reality as a unitary whole, as a "field." While reflexive, judging consciousness is important, we must first turn to the pre-reflexive, pre-conceptual, pre-logical structures which are at the origin of experience, prior to any thought *about* experience. The categories which Heidegger elaborates are those which *define* human existence as such, man as capable of experiencing and hence as capable of thinking about the world.

In this Sartre and Merleau-Ponty are true Heideggerians, without ever ceasing to be rigorously faithful to the phenomenological method of Husserl. The notions of consciousness and of intentionality are simply enlarged. It is not only the mind of man which is intentionally related to the world (which would actually be a reintroduction of an implicit body-mind dualism); it is man himself, as a concrete, living, experiencing, thinking, perceiving, imagining, willing, loving, hating, communicating being who is intentional of the world. Sartre's "existential psychoanalysis" and Merleau-Ponty's phenomenology of perception simply develop given lines of Heideggerian Daseinanalytics. And, it must be added, from a phenomenological point of view their work has only begun. They have blazed the way and made some progress along the path of establishing a radically new metaphysics of experience (what Heidegger calls *Fundamentalontologie*). We are not prejudging here to what extent Heidegger's or Sartre's or Merleau-Ponty's conclusions are wholly or in part justified or justifiable; we are simply trying to indicate with some clarity the direction of their phenomenological research.

Superficial readers have taken Husserl for an "essentialist" and an "idealist" and have wondered how such a modest and "inoffensive" epistemologist could be responsible for existentialism. But Husserl's philosophy is more explosive than such persons could imagine. Husserl was fully aware of this. Though his interests were those of a logician and epistemologist, he clearly laid the basis for a revolutionary metaphysics of experience—at least as revolutionary as Kantianism, which marked the rebirth of continental philosophy after the aridity of the Enlightenment, at least as revolutionary as Bergsonism, which marked the rebirth of French philosophy after the excesses of late nineteenth-century positivism. The chief merit of Thévenaz' essays on phenomenology is that they clearly show the continuity (in problematic and method) from Husserl to Merleau-Ponty.

Another difference between phenomenological transcendentalism and that of earlier philosophy must be noted.

Since it is a question of studying the structures of experience, there can be no question of limiting such analysis to the universally necessary and objectively valid structures of consciousness. These are, of course, extremely important and the lesson of phenomenology is that such structures, more fundamental than the Kantian categories, can be disclosed and thematized. But phenomenology is a radical empiricism and is concerned with the fullness of experience in its total, concrete, existential density. There are, according to Husserl, many kinds of life-worlds, and therefore many kinds of experiential-structures of life-experiencing-the-world. There is the impersonal (or pre-personal), public, taken-for-granted world within whose horizon we live our "natural" lives. There are more humanly and socially structured worlds of intersubjectivity, of language, of expression, and all forms of communication. There are the still more personally structured worlds of various social groups, cultures, historical epochs. Finally there are those incommunicable or imperfectly communicable worlds of private experience which each man possesses as his own.[25] For this reason the phenomenological elucidation of experience must be carried out on many different levels, as yet only very imperfectly distinguished. Phenomenology is thus a transcendentalism of a very special type, and it is precisely because of this richness and flexibility that it has already been able to illuminate in many ways the theoretical foundations of depth-psychology, psychoanalysis, social studies and other disciplines. There is not, in principle, any *phenomenon* (in the phenomenological sense of this term), or any area of human experience—from the universally valid categorial judgments of reflexive consciousness to the hidden pre-logical and pre-conceptual structures of the individual and collective subconscious—that falls outside the competence of phenomenological analysis. Like pragmatism, it is open to all kinds of human experience.

Husserl believed that he had established the foundations of a method of research which would have to be developed, applied, and extended by generations of philosophers. This explains why phenomenology among all the schools of contemporary philosophy manifests the most profound and striking diversity while claiming the unity of one method. It has already been able to furnish us with at least preliminary studies on the phenomenology of emotions (Scheler, Sartre, Strasser), aesthetics (Dufrenne), religion (Scheler, Van der Leeuw, Gusdorf), perception (Merleau-Ponty), imagination (Sartre), will (Ricoeur), of language and some areas of ethics. Yet, as Husserl foresaw, its work has only begun and fifty years after the "foundation of phenomenology" it is still impossible to define the phenomenological method in a simple manner, acceptable to all phenomenologists without qualification.

This, in itself, is hardly surprising. "Truly profound revolutions in philosophy," says Thévenaz, "proceed more from innovations of method than from metaphysical illuminations." Historical parallels are not wanting, both in the field of philosophy and elsewhere. It is inconvenient for those who believe that whatever can be stated can be stated clearly, but it is a fact of history that the great initiators seldom know very well themselves what they are doing when they launch their new method or new movement. When we think of Galileo and his fumbling attempts to state his "scientific method"—which was not *clearly* distinguished from philosophy or properly stated for nearly two centuries after his death—we can observe a case similar to Husserl's. Galileo *did* scientific research without being able to state clearly or thematically *what* he was doing. Phenomenology, in Husserl and in his successors, is in a similar position; it is by *doing* phenomenology that the phenomenological method itself becomes gradually clarified. Phenomenology is not the property of any one man, not even of Husserl; it is a legacy he has left to contemporary philosophers and it can only be defined in terms of the whole developing phenomenological tradition.

To return to Heidegger, one or two comments on Thévenaz' treatment of his later period are still necessary. The Heideggerian ontology of *Sein und Zeit* is clearly a philosophy of the this-side. The *Diesseitigkeit* is indeed fundamental to phenomenological research, conceived as the descriptive analysis of structures of experience. But already in his early period, and increasingly since 1950, Heidegger has turned his attention away from the study of existentials to the study of Being. He considers the existential analysis of the *Dasein* as a necessary but only a preliminary step. The *Dasein* is the being who asks the question of Being; it is through the *Dasein* that the question of Being (*Seinsfrage*) is made manifest. In short, the *Dasein* is the foundation of the possibility of the *experience* of beings and, hence, it can be called the "opening" of Being. But the *Dasein* is not the foundation of the *to be* of beings. For this reason, in his second period Heidegger has gone beyond his preliminary elaboration of the transcendental categories of experience (existentials) to the "contemplation" of the Being of beings.

This second period of Heidegger's philosophy has annoyed many people and Thévenaz seems to be among them. Has Heidegger simply escaped into mysticism? Is Being itself a "grace" as Thévenaz suggests? For those who have followed Heidegger into his second period such a suggestion does not seem very helpful. It is true that Heidegger's attempt to *think* the Being of beings, and later to let

Being be thought of itself—as it is "thought" and "named" in poetry, art, religious experience—is disconcerting in its results. As Parmenides and Plato found before him, Heidegger has discovered that the Being of beings does not permit one to "say" very much about it. What can be said, apparently, is that Being in Heidegger's philosophy is a "transcendental" in a very special and new sense. It is not a transcendental category of experience. It is not an existential. It is certainly not a "transcendental idea" in the Platonic or Scholastic sense. And Heidegger has told us explicitly that it is not God. But Heidegger has not told us what it *is,* and the reason is that he cannot. His vocabulary has become more and more personal, more and more powerful, and more and more obscure. He is attempting to think Being without using the traditional objectivist categories of Western philosophy, and thus has perforce fallen back on the more immediate, the more "lived" vocabulary of poetry and religion. It is clear that Heidegger's Being is not an abstraction; it is the very *to be* of beings, the ultimate ground not only of experience but of being. Perhaps those who find this period of Heidegger's thought "sterile" are right. At the very least, we must agree with Thévenaz that it is very unlikely that this aspect of Heidegger's thought will prove as fruitful or suggestive for phenomenological research as his Dasein-analytics. But we must be clear about one point: By going beyond the *Dasein* to the *Sein* of *Da-sein* (and all "beings") Heidegger believes himself to be pushing his original insights in a continuous direction to their ultimate foundations.

We find in what Thévenaz writes on this subject more than simple irritation with a style of thought which he believes to be sterile and obscurantist. It is an interesting fact that Heidegger's later philosophy has nearly as many opponents within the phenomenological tradition as outside it. If a man is to be judged by the quality of his enemies, as is sometimes the case, Heidegger ranks high. This is certainly an *ad hominem* argument, but it seems at least as justifiable as the opposite *ad hominem* which would dismiss the whole of Heidegger's thought because of his misguided and brief flirtation with the Nazi Party in 1933–1934, inexcusable as that may be. It may very well be true also that German professors of metaphysics are not as a rule very easy people to get along with; but this, in itself, is not sufficient reason to disregard what they have to say.[26]

Finally, we must qualify another point of Thévenaz' attack on the later Heidegger. When Thévenaz wrote these essays, Heidegger's writings on the phenomenology of language were just beginning to be published; indeed, even today we have only short and very incomplete samples from what appears to be a large unpublished corpus. Thévenaz may be correct in stating that Husserl "was not interested in language as such, in words." In one sense this is obviously true; Husserl was interested in experienced meanings and not in talk about experience. But it is inexact to say that he was uninterested in language as such, and on the basis of the little he did say on this subject Merleau-Ponty has been able to prepare the way for a very profound and fundamental investigation of language and the phenomenon of expression in general.[27] Heidegger follows his own route, but what he and Merleau-Ponty have written on language and expression goes far beyond the formal and logical analysis of the written and spoken word which up to now has constituted the twentieth-century contribution to the philosophy of language. This is not the place to justify such a claim or to recapitulate the present status of studies in the phenomenology of language. Suffice it to say that it differs profoundly from the logical analysis of language by going or attempting to go to the roots of the phenomenon of expression.

Husserl had already rejected the "algebraization" of meaning implicit in the forms of logical analysis he was acquainted with in his day. Words, for Husserl, are not simple, atomic, little "meanings" which can be exhaustively and adequately defined for use as "p's" and "q's" in an algebraized syllogism. Words are world-phenomena. If it is true that the primary structure of consciousness is intentionality, if man is inserted in the world, if he talks and acts, if he transforms the world and makes it "human," he does so *before he knows,* or before he can express to himself or to others what he is *doing.* The categories of *doing, being,* and *having* (as Sartre has shown) are all involved in the phenomenon of expression. In short, the phenomenon of expression is rooted very deeply in the primary preconscious structures of intersubjective experience. It is because man lives in the midst of things, next to things in the company of other men, and because he has a responsibility (Heidegger says "care") for beings that he speaks. Speech is one of the fundamental existentials in Heideggerian Dasein-analytics; it cannot be studied as a "natural" object in isolation from the total horizon of the lived experience of which it is a primary structure. It is not that phenomenology has any quarrel with the logical analysis of syntax and language, on the contrary—since "reason" or *logos* is also a root-phenomenon. But "logic" like any derived science must be situated with respect to its foundations in experience. The phenomenon of expression cannot be reduced to *logos;* it is both more fundamental and more general. Man acts and speaks *before he knows.*[28] Or, better, it is *by acting* and *in action* that he is enabled *to know.*

In conclusion, it is necessary to say something of the "pragmatism" of phenomenology. Thévenaz has pointed out that phenomenological existentialism (as distinguished from non-phenomenological or existentiel existentialism) is a "pragmatism." It is somewhat embarrassing that European scholars have had to point this out.[29] This aspect of phenomenology is certainly clearest in writers like Sartre and Merleau-Ponty, but it will not be missed by the perceptive and sympathetic reader of Husserl and Heidegger. It is less a case of direct or indirect influences[30] than a case of converging results and similar methodological approaches. It is precisely for this reason that the similarities between American pragmatism (especially the pragmatism of William James) and contemporary European phenomenology are so striking: they developed almost wholly independent of one another. Without attempting to be in any way exhaustive, let us simply note some of the points on which the theory of consciousness, the theory of man, and the theory of action implicit in pragmatism and phenomenology converge.

Aron Gurwitsch has brilliantly developed some of the basic themes of William James' theory of consciousness and shown their relevance for phenomenological analysis. In so doing he has shown—in French—that it is possible to discuss the field-theory of consciousness in the American terminology of William James. But we can go further. James defined his philosophy as a *radical empiricism,* by which he meant a metaphysics of experience of the same kind we have been discussing in phenomenology. He did not, of course, anticipate Husserl's phenomenological method, but he clearly aimed his philosophy in a convergent direction; if pragmatism had not been made so quickly into a simple "naturalistic" philosophy of "scientific invention and progress," and if it had not immediately afterwards fallen into the hands of formal logicians, inimical to empiricism, it would not have taken so long for this to become apparent.[31]

Also, James' "nativism" seems to have been an original attempt to elucidate the "transcendental" pre-conscious structures of lived perception with which phenomenology has made us familiar. It is not a question here of "innate" forms or ideas, structures of the perceiving *subject,* but rather a question of certain "open" structures which arise *in* experience. Certainly James was ahead of the psychology of his time, European as well as American, in his emphasis on the pre-conscious, the pre-reflexive, the pre-conceptual roots of thought and action.

The primacy of *action* as the fundamental category of early pragmatism gives us a notion of man-in-the-world, of an incarnate, unitary, intentional consciousness continuous with the notion of the intentionality of consciousness which is the basic discovery of phenomenology. Consciousness is less a type of "seeing" than of "acting." It is *praxis* before it can become *theoria.* James resolutely opposed the metaphysics of empiricism (Hume) and naturalism (Spencer). While he was also wary of "transcendentalism," it is because he knew only Kant and Hegel. But, reading James today is a refreshing experience. His philosophy, no less than Husserl's, was a return to experience, a turning from the abstract and derived categories of scientific constructions to the life-world in which they are rooted. Insofar as pragmatism as a philosophy of experience (in all its complexity and richness) is a living current in American thought, there remains the hope that William James, in death as in life, may bridge the impassable gulf that separates European from British-American philosophy.

These reflections are not written with a view to "gaining allies" for phenomenology in the American-speaking world. It will not do to gloss over the important differences between James' pragmatism and phenomenology. And these differences are not all in favor of phenomenology. It is not my view that William James stumbled "by accident" onto some of the "truths" of phenomenology. As a discoverer and initiator of a radically empirical philosophy, he is at least as important as Husserl. Like Husserl, he was a "perpetual debutante" in philosophy and his importance as the founder of pragmatism lies in the fact that his fundamental insights are capable of infinite development in the direction he laid down. Neither in Husserl nor in James do we find a "closed system." We find a method and a spirit of philosophical reflexion which, because of their radicalism, because of their faithfulness to experience, appear to be on convergent paths. It is not a question of trying to translate phenomenology and existentialism into the "respectable" Victorian terminology of William James. It is a question of recognizing the fundamental continuity of these two methods on many points and of stating clearly that the future of philosophy may lie in the direction of an *existential pragmatism*.

JAMES M. EDIE
Northwestern University

WHAT IS PHENOMENOLOGY?

THIS QUESTION IS as irritating for the layman who hearing the word would like to know at least roughly what it means, as it is for the historian of philosophy or the philosophical specialist who has the feeling of pursuing an elusive doctrine, never clearly defined during the fifty years of its rich evolution, which from Husserl leads through Scheler, Heidegger, Sartre, and many others up to Merleau-Ponty. Phenomenology seems to be a Proteus which appears now as an objective inquiry into the logic of essences and meanings, now as a theory of abstraction, now as a deep psychological description or analysis of consciousness, now as speculation on "the transcendental Ego," now as a method for approaching concretely lived existence, and finally, as in Sartre and Merleau-Ponty, seems to blend purely and simply with existentialism.

By now the skein is, to say the least, a bit tangled. However, it would be too easy to discredit phenomenology simply by accusing it of obscurity or confusion. A philosophy which after fifty years is still incapable of defining itself in a clear and univocal manner would stand accused by that very fact of an irremediable inconsistency! In reality we must conclude exactly the opposite. If a method originally forged for a very particular and limited end has been able to take on so many varying forms, it is because it holds

within itself a latent truth and efficacy, a power of renewal,
a principle of progress which attests to an exceptional fecundity. Further, does not a good part of this obscurity
come from our incapacity to hold on to all of these threads
at once and to discern the profound unity of the diverse
philosophies which claim the title of phenomenology?

Here we are verifying, moreover, that truly profound
revolutions in philosophy proceed more from innovations
of method than from metaphysical illuminations. At the
same time, we observe once again that what is originally
conceived as a purely methodological innovation, without
presuppositions, carries with it fundamental metaphysical
options which sooner or later are bound to manifest themselves. The value of the method will then show itself to be
strictly proportionate to the breadth of the philosophy or
to the number of philosophies it has inspired and nour-
ished.

In this connection we inevitably recall the stimulus
given by the Cartesian Method, which was meant at first to
be nothing but a method, but which within less than a century had given birth to three or four metaphysical systems
that Descartes himself would have been insulted to hear
called "Cartesian," and which were already tearing each
other apart. Kant's critical method also led to an astonishing metaphysical efflorescence and to the great post-kantian
and post-hegelian brawls. In 1800 or in 1840 it would have
been really difficult to define in a univocal formula acceptable to all thinkers just what was the decisive contribution
or the essence of the Copernican Revolution of Kant's Critique.

Nevertheless, if the skein of phenomenology is particularly tangled, this is due to the specific character of this
doctrine. The Cartesian Method was given at once in its
completed form, straightforward in its intention, simple in

its application; and Kant's critical method, after the dilatory researches of the pre-critical period, emerged fully matured and sure of itself. Husserl, however, and phenomenology itself, winds and gropes its way, constantly retracing its steps, probing the unseen ground before it, continually putting everything in question. We can say that phenomenology paradoxically unites two qualifications, reputedly exclusive of one another: it is methodical and groping.

And there is more. The disconcerting productivity of Husserl, who without respite filled more than forty thousand pages out of which he chose only a few samples for publication during his lifetime (and even these received constant revision and reworking), has created the delicate situation in which the historian of philosophy finds himself. Even before Husserl himself knew exactly where he was going and what he was really searching for, his resolute step and the sterling quality of his method had already caught up and carried along a number of thinkers and philosophers. Thus, during the period in which Husserl himself was going through his gravest crisis of interior doubt and incertitude, there already existed a group of disciples, each running as fast as he could down a different track, each with his own temperament and problems (Scheler, Geiger, Pfänder, etc.). Then, at a later stage of Husserl's evolution, it was transcendental phenomenology that gave rise to new inquiries, for example those of Heidegger. But Heidegger eclipsed his master and at once transformed him into a figure of the past, belonging only to the history of philosophy. Such is the fate of the great initiators: even before publishing his final works a Kant, a Bergson, a Husserl is already "historical," "left behind"; his own posterity lowers the curtain.[1]

Moreover, extra-philosophical factors contributed to ac-

celerate the premature obsolescence of Husserl. In the Nazi
Germany of 1930–1940 Husserl's work was drowned in
silence because he was a Jew,[2] and he died in oblivion in
1938. The tragedy is that this throwing into the past and
this oblivion is irremediable. In spite of the current publication of the *Husserliana,* it does not seem that the down-
hill course can be reversed. Husserl's thought, at least in
Germany, now interests only historians of philosophy, and
yet it is only now beginning to be known and understood
in its totality and in its unity. We can see him as the
founder of phenomenology and honor him as such, but it
is not with him that we feel we ought to initiate ourselves
to phenomenology today; our attention is turned to Heidegger and his school, and in France to Sartre and Merleau-
Ponty.

I THE PHENOMENOLOGY OF HUSSERL

The Unity and Signification of Husserlian Philosophy

To understand Husserl's phenomenology it is necessary, first of all, to avoid taking each of his works in isolation and treating them merely as successive applications of
an original method to various subjects: logic, time, structure of consciousness, evidence, intentionality, crisis of the
sciences, etc. Nor should one attempt to see in them, as in
Leibniz, only a succession of points of view all expressing
the same fundamental intuition in different ways. On the
contrary, we must see them as a patient attempt to clarify
what is seen at first only obscurely and hesitatingly; this is
so true that Husserl's later works are to a large extent indispensable to a correct understanding of his earlier writings (rather than vice versa). It is necessary to read or at

least to interpret Husserl backwards[3] or, better yet, in zig-zag.[4] Otherwise, like Husserl's first disciples who found in the *Logische Untersuchungen* a fruitful method and a sane realism only to be scandalized later on by the idealism of the *Ideen,* we will seem to find in Husserl's evolution breaks, unintelligible about-faces, and all sorts of inconsistencies that exist only in our imagination.

Let us try, from the beginning, to place ourselves at the heart of his thought, at that crossroads of seemingly incompatible data and demands. Here is a philosopher whose first concern is to cut completely the ties between logic and psychology, and who then seems to return endlessly to psychology and the analysis of consciousness in order to found his logic and his phenomenology. Or again, here is a realist whose revolutionary impact, in the context of the neokantian idealism of the end of the nineteenth century, consisted precisely in his "Wendung zum Objekt" (turning to the object) and in his famous "Zu den Sachen selbst" (to the things themselves), but who considered his most urgent task to lie in analyzing the subject, consciousness, and in elaborating a transcendental idealism. What does this mean?

The problem that haunted Husserl from his *Philosophie der Arithmetik* (1891) until his death was that of foundations. This is the guiding thread of his thought and it shows us the unity of the prodigious effort of reflexion that made of this mathematician one of the greatest philosophers of the twentieth century. Questioning himself on the foundations of mathematics, he is sent back to logic, then to epistemology, then to ontology, and even to the philosophy of history by an irrepressible movement of perpetually going-beyond. This is one of the most striking characteristics of this philosophy of the intentional dynamism of consciousness. But his goal remains identical from the

Logische Untersuchungen, where he is looking for "the new foundation of pure logic and epistemology" (I, vii), to the *Cartesian Meditations,* where he is preoccupied with "giving the sciences an absolute foundation." And very quickly Husserl recognizes that the sciences, in spite of the fact that their actual results are always approximative and imperfect, are oriented, in intention, towards an *absolute objectivity.* If science is truly worthy of the name, it is because of this aim, because of this *idea* of science and not because of its results or the content of scientific knowledge. There lies the meaning of science and it is from this perspective that any inquiry into the foundations of science must begin. Thus it is the intention of the scientist, which is to say the intentionality of consciousness, that must be analyzed; the foundation will not be found except on the side of the subject. We see here the double preoccupation of phenomenology: it will be at one and the same time a search for an absolutely objective foundation and an analysis of the subjectivity of consciousness.

But in 1900 whoever spoke of the analysis of consciousness spoke of psychology, for that was the moment when psychology reigned supreme. Now it seems evident that psychology is incapable of founding or even of clarifying the absolute objectivity inherent in the idea of science. Every psychological explanation tends fatally to destroy this absolute and to dissolve objectivity in a relativist subjectivism (and this is precisely what the first volume of the *Logische Untersuchungen* subjected to a critique which has now become classic).

Husserl, then, makes an attempt to open up a new direction in the analysis of consciousness. It is not psychological analysis because it aims essentially at answering the epistemological problem of the absolute foundation of logic and science. It is *phenomenological* analysis. What distinguishes it from logical or psychological analysis? Let us note first of all that it bears the mark of the mathematical mind that conceived it. The mathematician is used to manipulating ideal values or essences without ever having to ask himself whether or not they correspond to a factual reality. In the same way the phenomenologist does not, like the logician, study the conditions of a true judgment; nor, like the scientist, if it is true that . . .; nor, like the psychologist, what *effectively* goes on in consciousness; he rather asks the question: What do we mean by . . .? (Was *meinen* wir?). What is the *meaning* of what we have in mind when we judge, affirm, dream, live, etc. . . .? Phenomenology is never an investigation of external or internal facts. On the contrary, it silences experience provisionally, leaves the question of objective reality or of real content aside in order to turn its attention solely and simply on *the reality in consciousness,* on the objects insofar as they are intended by and in consciousness, in short on what Husserl calls ideal essences. By this we must not understand mere subjective representations (which would leave us on the plane of psychology) nor ideal *realities* (which would "reify" or hypostasize unduly the data of consciousness and would put us on the level of metaphysics), but precisely the *"phenomena."*

To understand this term we must completely forget the Kantian opposition between phenomenon and thing-in-itself; because, if phenomenology puts reality (in-itself) in parentheses, it cannot conceive the phenomenon in relation to an in-itself, as a reality of the second order, for us. The phenomenon here is that which manifests itself immediately in consciousness; it is grasped in an intuition that precedes any reflexion or any judgment. It has only to be allowed to show itself, to manifest itself; *the phenomenon is that which gives itself (Selbstgebung).* The phenomenological method then, faced with the objects and the contents of knowledge, consists in neglecting what alone counts for philosophers and scientists, namely, their value, their reality or unreality. It consists in describing them such as they give themselves, as pure and simple intentions [*visées*] of consciousness, as meanings, to render them visible and manifest as such. In this *Wesenschau,* the essence (*Wesen*) is neither ideal *reality* nor psychological reality, but ideal intention [*visée*], intentional object of consciousness, immanent to consciousness.

Husserl applied his new method first to the problem that preoccupied him, that of the foundation of logic; he tried to clear a path for "pure logic" between logicism and psychologism by isolating logical "phenomena" or logical "essences." But contemporaries saw very quickly that it was possible to use the phenomenological method to renew *every science of objects* on condition that one progress from empirical facts to phenomena to essences. A vast unexplored territory was opened up into which philosophers, weary of treading the beaten paths of positivism and scientism, literally rushed, without however abandoning a solid anti-metaphysical bias. In this way phenomenological descriptions accumulated and there quite rapidly appeared phenomenologies of law, of art, of religion, etc.

But Husserl, driven on by a rare philosophical élan, was already breaking through the limits of his method, whose horizons nevertheless appeared unlimited. His problem of the foundation allowed him no rest and, as he went into it more deeply, he discovered with increasing anxiety that this problem was in reality the problem of philosophy itself, or rather it was philosophy become problematic to itself. If there was a crisis of logic and the sciences, it was because there was first of all a crisis of philosophy. And the problem of the foundation, pushed beyond preparatory phenomenological inquiries, became the problem of the primary and radical foundation of philosophy. "Knowledge, which in ordinary pre-philosophical thought is the most natural thing in the world, suddenly emerges as a *mystery*."[5] If phenomenology does not manage to restore authentic philosophy, if it is not able to become this radical philosophy, it will have failed in its search for the foundations.

The description of the phenomena had opened up the way, but it was not able of itself to lead Husserl to his goal. In fact, it is clear that it would be contradictory to try to solve the problem of the foundation and, what is more, of the absolute foundation of rational knowledge by means of a merely descriptive method or by the intuition of essences. The phenomenological method concealed within itself an aim which was at first veiled but which gradually became more and more explicit. It was no longer only a matter of viewing and describing the simple "appearing" of things, neither was it a question of a theory of knowledge in the sense of the epistemology of the end of the nineteenth century. In fact, "the theory of the essence of knowledge"[6] will not be centered on the question of objectivity or of truth since reality and being are suspended. But on the new terrain of phenomenological analysis it will aim at renewing, once more starting from scratch, the problem of the radical foundation of the whole enterprise of philosophical reason. It will be a question of finding an absolute evidence which, like the "phenomenon," would justify itself, which would present itself as primary and absolute, in need of nothing outside itself to found it, in short, a radical source of "apodicticity" which would give to science and to reason in general their meaning.

In this way the phenomenological method, appropriate

to the descriptive analysis of essences intended [*visées*] by consciousness, must itself be radicalized. It is at this decisive moment that Husserl discovers and brings in the "phenomenological reduction," thus giving access on the philosophical level to a position which will still be neither objectivist (or naturalist), nor metaphysical, nor, it goes without saying, psychologistic or subjectivistic. A new field is opened up: the *transcendental* field. From a non-psychological analysis of consciousness, Husserl passes to the analysis of non-psychological consciousness, to transcendental consciousness. It is by a process of *reduction* (going against the natural tendencies of the mind), by a radical ascesis, by a total engagement, that he exorcises the spectre of psychology and the sly temptations of psychologism. Phenomenology then becomes a transcendental philosophy.

What is the meaning of the term transcendental here? And how does this new step help Husserl towards the solution of his problem?

The reduction is called "phenomenological" in the sense indicated above: this time it is to permit a grasping of *the world* (no longer simply such-and-such an object in the world) as *phenomenon*. It is not a question of making it appear in its factual reality or in its existence (which are put in parentheses), but in its immanent reality to consciousness. What is "reduced" is now—rather than facts or the "real" in such-or-such an area of knowledge—the world, the ensemble of all the empirical, rational, and even scientific judgments that we make about the world in the natural attitude. To reduce does not mean to eliminate or to put in doubt. There is nothing here similar to the skeptical stage that a Descartes crosses in order to recover later on, piece by piece, the world eliminated by doubt. The putting in parentheses, "the coefficient of nullity,"[7] attributed to the world, does not mean that Husserl detaches himself from the world and plunges it, like Descartes, momentarily into non-being. All to the contrary, the primordial and essential purpose of the reduction is to bring to light this essential intentional contact between consciousness and the world, a relationship which in the natural attitude remains veiled. For Husserl, in the reduction the world remains where it is, but now one perceives that every act of knowledge in fact refers to a subject (the transcendental Ego) as to an ultimate and primary term which is the origin, the support or foundation of its meaning.

The reduction leads then simultaneously to "the apodictic evidence" of the *I* (to the *cogito,* to the consciousness of self) and to the world-phenomenon intended by this transcendental consciousness, and above all to their absolutely fundamental and indissoluble conjunction (intentionality of the transcendental consciousness). But this *cogito* is not, as with Descartes, the indubitable knowledge of a *being,* of a thinking *thing* which "holds steady" in a dubitable world, nor is it the interior experience of a sort of primitive fact, the ego. That would be to remain on the level of the world, of psychological knowledge, and of the natural knowledge of fact. It is the grasping of self outside of the natural world, in an absolutely indubitable evidence, as transcendental subjectivity, that is to say as origin of all meanings, as the sense of the world. Likewise, to make the world appear as phenomenon is to understand that the being of the world is no longer its existence or its reality, but its meaning, and that this meaning of the world resides in the fact that it is a *cogitatum* intended by the *cogito.* The reduction reveals not the *cogito* alone but *ego-cogito-cogitatum,*[8] that is to say, consciousness-of-the-world, consciousness constituting the meaning of the world. And the world, in this new perspective, "is not an existence but a simple phenomenon,"[9] it is signification. Let us not imagine then two spheres which divide the whole of reality: the natural world and the transcendental field, which would be like a metaphysical ulterior-world [*arrière-monde*] susceptible in its turn of being described, grasped, known as a second nature. There is only one world and the transcendental is rather, it seems to me, another name for the constituting intentionality of consciousness.

We ought, if we had time, to show here in detail how the notion of *intentionality* fundamentally transforms the traditional data of the philosophical problem. In Franz Brentano the notion of intentionality did not yet have more than a psychological bearing; it was the characteristic mark of all psychic phenomena. In Husserl it has from the beginning an epistemological bearing, then transcendental, even ontological: it characterizes a new relationship between the subject and the object, between thought and being, an essential relationship whereby these are inseparable and without which neither consciousness nor the world could be grasped. The intentionality of consciousness signifies that "all consciousness is consciousness of something," but, of course, it is not a question here of that frequently mentioned banality according to which all consciousness or knowledge has an object or a content! After the centuries men have spent reflecting on knowledge, we hardly have need at this date of making such a "discovery." No, by virtue of intentionality the very notion of a reality in itself or of an absolute object becomes absurd, and in any case unthinkable.[10] And, on the other hand, the idea (of Descartes, for example) of a consciousness closed in on itself, which would not perceive the world *itself* and whose first job would be to make certain that it perceived reality "in the original," is likewise excluded. By the same token, the task of philosophy can no longer consist in anxiously installing itself in the bosom of the natural existing world and natural consciousness, between the subject and the object, in a "critical" attitude whose aim would be to establish whether or not the subject attains objectivity in itself, whether the object is seen or constructed by the subject, which would question itself concerning the reality of the external world, etc.[11] "Philosophy is placed in a *new dimension* with regard to all natural knowledge . . . and to this new dimension corresponds a new *method,* radically new, opposed to the 'natural' method. To deny this would be to have misunderstood the nature of the problems proper to the critique of knowledge, to have misunderstood what philosophy wants and ought to be . . ."[12] And Husserl adds: "It may seem pretentious for me to dare address a reproach of such gravity, the most serious that can be addressed to present philosophy and indeed to any philosophy of the past, even when it admits that philosophy has its own methods. But silence serves nothing where essentials are at stake, even if I have to give the impression of pretentiousness."[13]

In order to clarify this discovery let us try to see in transcendental intentionality an original bringing together of Cartesian themes (evidence, intuition, in short, viewing) and Kantian themes (the constitution of the object in consciousness, thus *the constituting or creative activity of consciousness*). Even though Husserl speaks a Kantian language, particularly in his first exposition of the reduction (*Die Idee der Phänomenologie*), we must not be misled. His radicalism may very well be transcendental; his inspiration is much less Kantian than Cartesian. Going against the whole German anti-Cartesian tradition, Husserl attaches himself to the radical aim that motivates the experience of the methodic doubt. Though he defines phenomenology as *"a critique of* logical and practical *reason,"*[14] he does not mean at all, like Kant, to call reason before the bar to verify its titles and pretensions, but rather to attack the mystery of knowledge at its roots.

Like Kant, Husserl thinks that the object refers to the subject and that the problem of knowledge is essentially a problem of *constitution:* it is by beginning with (transcendental and non-psychological) consciousness that we will be able to comprehend the structures of the intentional world and, above all, the unity of its meaning. But, like Descartes, Husserl sees consciousness not merely as the formal and unifying element of knowledge, the condition for the possibility of the object, but as a concrete (non-empirical) datum, immediately lived as consciousness (but not in the psychological sense). The object is not *constructed* by this consciousness; it gives itself or reveals itself to the view of this consciousness. Here we go boldly beyond any realism or idealism (whether psychological or subjectivistic) thanks to this notion of *Selbstgebung* which brings together the Cartesian theme of intuition and the Kantian theme of constitution. We are able to make this advance because all transcendentalism, and especially that of Husserl, implies it. Phenomenology invites us to make a sort of *transcendental seeing*[15] or *transcendental experience.* This resolute return to the evidence, after all the constructivisms of neo-kantianism, is first of all a return to the apodictic evidence with which consciousness grasps itself in the *cogito.* Secondly, this consciousness "lives" itself immediately as the giver of sense, as the source of meaning for the world. And finally, in this double evidence the object or the thing (the world) is *already given,* essentially tied to consciousness by intentionality. In other words, the world gives itself to consciousness which confers on it its meaning.

This stratum of transcendental evidences is rendered accessible by the reduction, which reveals its true countenance. It is much more than a simple method or technique; it is a turning-around of intentionality. Instead of losing ourselves in the intended object, we reflect on the intentional act. We take a new attitude in relation to the world of our experience and thus open up a new field of *experience* by bringing to light a new consciousness, because this transcendental Ego is not an empty and formal ego, but a concrete ego. We must insist here again on the permanence of Husserl's anti-psychologism even on the transcendental plane. If the transcendental plane is a field of experience, something concrete and lived, it is not some kind of rare experience, some unheard of subtlety of intimate experience of self, but actually a non-psychological domain: that of *meaning,* of the apodictic foundation, of a true rational and philosophical evidence. Let us say rather that this domain is that of the *consciousness of meaning* (which is necessarily consciousness giving meaning), and that this transcendental experience is rationality itself, called to consciousness and comprehension of itself, conquering the creative intuition of the sense that it carries implicitly within itself.

We see, in consequence, the double task of the phenomenological reduction. (1) It must, on the one hand, definitively put aside the renascent temptations of psychological consciousness, permit us to go beyond its irremediable contingency and the various relativisms which ruin any search for meaning and foundation, and thus bring us to the apodictic evidence of the radical foundation. (2) On the other hand, it guards us from any naive realism or naturalism. Intentionality likewise has a double merit: (1) to explode idealism by projecting consciousness towards the world, by placing it in the world, and (2) to assure the connection between contingent lived experience and the necessary meaning of this lived experience.

The method of reduction therefore permitted Husserl to carry ahead his phenomenological description and even to ask of it the solution to the problem of the radical foundation. He has the right, consequently, to say that phenomenology is "first philosophy"[16] in the double sense of an essentially inceptive, beginning philosophy, and of a philosophy of the fundamental principles. But for once, first philosophy and experience (in the non-empirical meaning Husserl gives the term) are not mutually exclusive. This first philosophy, which henceforth does not fear to call itself metaphysics, remains a "radical empiricism."[17] In fact, in spite of all the reductions, all the putting in parentheses, lived experience remains intact and present up to the end, and especially the primary and indestructible contact of consciousness with lived experience. One cannot even speak of a "return to lived experience" via the reduction, because, in fact, we have never left it. But now we live it and see it differently by learning to see it in its meaning, in its apodicticity, in its fundamental rationality.

At this radical level empiricism and rationalism are no longer exclusive of one another. The manifestation of the *Lebenswelt* in which transcendental phenomenology culminates, this grandiose consecration of lived experience as the radical foundation of philosophy, is completely faithful to the original intention of phenomenology, animated like Bergsonism by a profound respect for the real. This consecration of lived experience is not the work of a more or less irrational vitalism; it grew out of the rational demands of the logician, of an austerely intellectualist philosophy which implacably reduces the psychological, the vital, the empirical, the relative. But this primacy of lived experience enables us to understand the continuity of Husserl's thought with post-husserlian phenomenology and with certain forms of existentialism.

It is not possible to stop experiencing the world—not even, and especially not, when one reflects on it, for reflexion is still a way of intending the world. Philosophy is involved in life, and when one imagines that it is detaching itself, it is because it is living the world differently, more intensely. The lived world is therefore never foreign to reason for Husserl; it is only that reason remains too often latent and requires much effort and many ruptures to make it appear. This is why coming to full consciousness of the meaning of the world and of the meaning of reason (these are one and the same) remains an infinite task for philosophy. But even if Husserl, at the end of his life, felt himself to be more than ever a "beginner," and still aspired to begin everything all over again *ab ovo,* philosophy, finally conscious of itself and radically founded thanks to phenomenology, was in his eyes the only *raison d'être* of humanity, and its chance of salvation.

II THE PHENOMENOLOGY OF HEIDEGGER

1. From Phenomenology to Ontology

It is undeniable that at its beginnings phenomenology was anti-metaphysical. Against the systems it advocated a method, against all metaphysical speculation or construction, a philosophy that would be "rigorous science,"[18] against intemperate metaphysical realism it proceeded to a salutary putting in parentheses of judgments of existence and reality. Phenomenology thus installed itself in a metaphysically neutral zone, where "the things themselves" show themselves and give themselves before any intervention of the mind.

Is this to say that phenomenology was oriented towards

phenomenalism (the phenomenon conceived as the only reality)? Not at all, for, as we have said, the phenomenon, according to Husserl, is not opposed to being; it is not a thing for-us opposed to a thing in-itself; it is not a lesser reality, nor an appearance, nor a simple representation. Moreover, if the central preoccupation of Husserl's phenomenology is the search for the radical and primary foundation of all knowledge, and if Husserl pushed this search in a transcendental direction, it is clear that this philosophy requires a general theory of being, an ontology. Phenomenology, then, was animated from the very beginning, and this quickly became more than a purely latent element, by an ontological concern. It was polarized in the direction of a new metaphysics and little by little became aware that its job was precisely to lay the foundations for it. To the degree that phenomenology developed, it became increasingly clear that it had been from the beginning an ontology which, because of its very novelty, needed time to recognize itself as such. By this continual movement of going-beyond and of progressive explication, phenomenology very naturally discovered and uncovered the ontology which sustained it and towards which it was tending. This was already apparent in Husserl;[19] it became fully explicit in Heidegger.

In treating Husserl's evolution from his early phenomenology to transcendental phenomenology, we called attention to the fact that some of his disciples viewed this as an about-face from realism to idealism. In Heidegger, and later in Sartre, phenomenology has been accused of renouncing itself and becoming ontology. But if we do not lose sight of the permanence of the problem at stake and the unquestionable continuity of the method in its very development, we will find in this more and more marked coincidence of phenomenology and ontology, in this "phenomenological ontology," not a square circle or an unnatural union, but the originality and the depth of the new method.

However, the being which is in question now can no longer be that of Scholastic ontology or of Hegelian ontology. As for Husserl, Heidegger's question will not be to ask *what is there,* nor what reality can I know for certain, nor what is the primary and fundamental reality. The question will be: *What is the meaning of being?* What do we understand by being? Up to Heidegger there was a tacit agreement that the meaning of the word "being" was evident but undefinable. Heidegger, as an authentic phenomenologist, careful to distinguish meanings,[20] showed that if it is difficult to answer the question: What is the meaning of "being"? it is because the meaning of the question itself is unclear. What is closest to us is at the same time the most obscure. To bring it into light, to make it the theme of methodical investigation, that is the job of phenomenology. Happily, we already have at our disposal a certain vague comprehension of the word "is" which enables us to pose the question. Analysis ought to permit us to make this too summary meaning more explicit by bringing out little by little the structures and modes of being, by "bringing into view . . . that which at first and in most cases is not shown" or "remains hidden" (*verborgen*).[21]

We do not propose to retrace the main lines of Heidegger's ontology (excellent critical studies already exist in French), but to show the phenomenological orientation of his inquiry, its extension, and its results. First of all, we find the distinctive signs of the phenomenological method: a method of "showing" (*Aufweisung*), or uncovering or laying bare (*Freilegung*), of making explicit (*Auslegung*) which is meant to bring to light the "forgotten" being, to rediscover what lay covered or entombed. This "hermeneutics" is clearly in the line of the transcendental phenomenology of Husserl's *Ideen*.[22] It is a question of isolating the fundamental structures of being which are the "conditions of possibility" of our empirical world, which are the constitutive foundations of all that is. —We find furthermore the opposition of the real and its meaning, the empirical and the transcendental, in the form of the opposition which is the key to *Sein und Zeit* between the ontic (that which is, the existent, *das Seinde*) and the ontological (being or the meaning of what is, *das Sein*). —We find, finally, in an even more intensified form if that is possible, the search for a truly radical foundation, not only of knowledge as with Husserl, but of the quality of being of all that is: a foundation which is a meaning. Heideggerian ontology is a *Fundamentalontologie,* that aims at answering *the* fundamental question _(*Fundamentalfrage*): What is the meaning of being? and at revealing a *Fundamentalstruktur.*[23]

Heidegger has a passion for questioning. Perhaps only Aristotle can be compared to him in the astonishing ability he has to pose problems, to question beyond still premature answers, and beneath questions that are never radical enough. If philosophy is the art or the mania of posing questions where everything is self-evident, and by preference where nothing seems problematic, then Heidegger is the most philosophical of philosophers. Behind the questions he is going back indefatigably towards an ever more fundamental foundation.[24] The radicalism of this quest is shown by the fact that this *Fragen* is an incessant *Zurükfragen.*[25]

In Husserl the search for a radical foundation led to transcendental or constituting consciousness (constitutive source of everything intended by the intentionality of this consciousness). The foundation was expressed in terms of consciousness. In Heidegger interrogation pushes still deeper, even below transcendental consciousness, down to the "foundation of the foundation."[26] And it is already evident that this "iteration," this redoubling of radicalism can lead us only to a sort of "void without ground" (*Ab-grund*), toward a nothingness,[27] a nothingness more radical than any being or than any foundation that is (that is to say, which would be only a "being"). Fundamental ontology leads into an ontology of non-being, into a *méontologie*.[28]

The essential originality of Heidegger's transcendentalism in relation to that of his master Husserl is its attempted resolution of the problem of the foundation without recourse to consciousness, not even transcendental consciousness, which was no doubt still too "idealist," too "subjectivist" in his eyes. He bases himself on a more clearly ontological structure beneath the level of consciousness, the *Dasein*, from which alone one is able to understand the possibility and the meaning of a consciousness or of a transcendental Ego.

What is the Dasein? It has become customary to translate it by "human reality" (Corbin, Sartre) or "human existence" (De Waelhens) in order to avoid the too bloodless and abstract "to-be-there." This is somewhat unfortunate in that we are carried towards anthropology, towards existentiel and concrete man, while Heidegger is oriented in the diametrically opposite direction, since he goes beyond not only the empirical and psychological towards the transcendental but even beyond consciousness towards something less personal and more ontological.[29] The *there* of the to-be-there does not express simple factual existence; nor does it indicate a place, but rather indicates, below the level of empirical data, that which renders it possible that something exists or is present in a certain place. As W. Biemel[30] has very rightly put it, the *there* is a fundamental structure by means of which man is open onto something. It is on the most radically ontological level, as "irruption" or as "opening up of the open,"[31] that the Dasein and consequently man will finally be able to be understood in that which gives meaning to their being. In an unpublished course of 1929[32] Heidegger explains that the *Da* is *"ein Umkreis von Offenbarkeit,"* an area of revealability, an area of opening up where something can manifest itself (as "phenomenon").

"Daseinsanalytics," by revealing this possibility of opening up, clears the way to hidden and forgotten being and constitutes the original phenomenological method of Heideggerian ontology. The vague and summary comprehension of the meaning of *is* renders radical ontological questioning possible. Man's preoccupation with being, with this dim little light of comprehension, will permit (as a reminiscence) the revealing of being. It is in this sense and in this sense alone that the first step, in *Sein und Zeit,* consists in going from man to being, and that the human "care" for being (*Sorge*) can be taken as the key which opens being for us. We see why in this first book Heidegger proposes only a preliminary analysis: he does not yet speak of being itself but unfolds the whole field of the *ontological* structures of human existence (being-in-the-world, care, temporality, historicity, affective tonality, etc.). It is here that the decisive influence of Kierkegaard makes itself felt, but it is important to see that the *existentiel*[33] and vital themes of the Danish philosopher (anguish, possibility, repetition, decision, etc.) are immediately transposed into a transcendental and ontological register. In Heidegger they represent the *existential*[33] structures of the Dasein which itself is an eminently ontological structure. Even while utilizing Kierkegaard, phenomenological transcendentalism squarely opposes the philosophy of existence understood as the analysis of existing man on the level of lived experience and the concrete. Compared to the existentiel[33] philosophy of the kind represented by Kierkegaard, Jaspers, or Gabriel Marcel, the *existential*[33] phenomenology of Heidegger is distinguished from the beginning by the loss (provisional at least) or the putting in parentheses of *concrete man*, similar to Husserl's (provisional?) loss or suspension of [psychological] *consciousness*. In order to reveal being, obscured by what is, it is necessary to operate this kind of phenomenological reduction of man and consciousness.

Let us not say, therefore, that Heidegger's ontology is based on an anthropology; it is preferable to avoid expressions like philosophy of existence, "privilege of the ego," or "of man."[34] Henceforth, since it is being which reveals itself, and since truth is really, according to its Greek etymology, "the hidden being which reveals itself" (*a-létheia*, ά-λήθεια, *Unverborgenheit*), *Being* manifests its unconditional primacy, which will be indicated in the rest of this article by writing it with a capital. But it must not be forgotten that it is always a question of Being-meaning and not of the metaphysical and transcendent reality of the supreme Being of classical philosophy.

2. *The Transcending or Abandonment of Phenomenology: Being and Language*

Heidegger's most recent writings,[35] rare fragments of a large unpublished corpus which the master of Freiburg somewhat haughtily refuses to communicate to anyone outside his circle of initiates and devoted disciples,[36] emphasize very clearly this primacy of Being and give the final (or at least the present) sense of the whole Heideggerian enterprise. As an authentic phenomenologist, Heidegger up to now was uncovering being starting from man, as Husserl unfolded the world from intentional consciousness. But just as we ultimately came to the primacy of the lived world in Husserl, we now see in Heidegger that the relation between man and Being is reversed and takes on its real and definitive signification. Instead of man revealing Being, it is Being which *opens* itself and gives itself, and the Dasein, "opening up of the open," will represent henceforth the opening of Being to man. Heidegger qualifies this with increasing insistence as an event or an advent (*Ereignis, Ereignung*).[37]

But this reversed relationship or this displacement of the center of gravity, which seems so similar to the one we noted in Husserl, unfolds very different consequences and leads apparently to an abandonment of the phenomenological method. Let us try to understand why.

Up to this point the turning from being to Being, similar to Husserl's "reduction," operated like a putting in parentheses of the world of beings which permitted a more explicit grasp of Being. But now the key to the Being-man relationship is no longer, for Heidegger, human questioning, the care of Being, in short the intentionality or the project (*Entwurf*) of the Dasein. Heidegger sacrifices completely the existentiel and anthropological language of Kierkegaard that he attempted to transpose in *Sein und Zeit* (this was then only a provisional crutch to open up the way to Being). He begins from above: it is Being, conceived as a kind of obscure and hidden power, that consents to manifest itself, that marks out itself the place of its opening, that condescends thus to give itself to man, like a kind of grace, to come out of itself, to express itself, to make itself meaningful. Patient phenomenological inquiry, with its indefinitely protracted and repeated preliminaries, is suddenly cut short; there is no longer a method. For, if Being comes to man, or rather if, in opening itself up, it gives rise to the *Da* and thereby to the very possibility of man, man is no longer required to stir himself, to clear his way. The passion for method, still so visible in *Sein und Zeit,* this pathos of infinite exploration inherited from Husserl, vanishes. One perceives now that the much sought-after radical foundation is within one's possession, at least under the form of disclosures—or of revelations—as brilliant as they are fleeting. Thus we see here very clearly the consequences of evicting the Husserlian consciousness. If Being in Heidegger becomes the object of human intentionality, this will only be in a derivative manner; it will itself first pose the intentional human consciousness that intends it. Being is no longer a transcendental foundation (for there is no transcendental except for a consciousness that is the source of meaning, constitutive of the world); it tends to become once more simply transcendent. As much to say that the world of Being and of meanings ceases to be the human world to which phenomenology had accustomed us.

The accent which was on the concern for being now passes to language, the new center of the Being-man relationship since Being opens, exteriorizes, expresses itself. But that precisely which speaks is no longer man; it is Being. It sends forth a cry into the desert in order to stimulate the echo which will send back its solitary Word. It is Being that creates for itself the ear destined to hear and the words that carry its revelation. In observing this importance given to language we might be inclined to think that Heidegger is in the line of phenomenological inspiration. Inquiry into significations led phenomenology in fact to the heart of the problem of language and to a renewal of the philosophy of language.[38] But what a difference there is between Husserl and the latest form of Heidegger's philosophy. Husserl sought for meanings in the framework of the intentionality of consciousness, as ideal realities or essences; he was not interested in language as such, in words. He studied language as the signifying behavior of man and meanings as "phenomena."[39] In return, Heidegger since *Sein und Zeit* has done a sort of phenomenology of words. By manipulating etymologies, by "reducing" the everyday meaning of words, by exploding them, he tries to disclose their implicit or buried meanings, to recover human language at its meaningful source. But if the meanings which reveal themselves now as objective realities are words recharged from a fullness of lost meaning, this is as much as to say that language is no longer the instrument that man uses to express himself, but the very revelation of Being. "Language is not something that man, among other faculties or instruments, *also possesses,* but *that which possesses man.*"[40] Even before man thinks or speaks, Being speaks to man and renders language, logic, and thought possible.

But we see to what an extent the method and ambition of phenomenology has been attenuated. This "voice of Being,"[41] this "non-spoken word,"[42] this ontological language is no longer the bearer of human meanings; it is a sort of sacred language or mysterious symbol, a sort of revelation of Being in the absence of all human words. The philosopher, in the current sense of the term, should keep silent; it is the poet and the "thinker" who will replace him. They have the word, or rather the word has them. The poet, confidant of Being, having learned to "exist in that which has no name,"[43] is able *"to name* the sacred." As for the thinker, he is able *"to speak* Being."[44] We understand Heidegger's present predilection for the ontological-philological exegesis of the poets (notably Hölderlin) and for the first pre-socratics who *spoke* Being as one religiously recites a sacred formula.

The reader of Heidegger stumbles on every page over the orthographical contrivances that attempt to mould as best they can the evolution of meanings. Yet one must recognize the astonishing power of expression and suggestion of this philosophical language. *Ek-sistenz* enables us to avoid the ambiguities of *Existenz; Seyn* shows the gulf between Heideggerian Being and the *Sein* of classical metaphysics. Words are no longer words; they cannot help bursting to manifest the presence of Being. Depositories of an ontological and superhuman message, they wrap themselves in an essential silence. Heidegger no longer pronounces them without a holy trembling, with a pathetic gravity, like oracles not to be divulged in the world of "das Man," but to be pondered in self-communion.

With Husserl, phenomenology was a continual going-beyond, but within the continuity of one method; here it is phenomenology itself that is surpassed. It had become metaphysics, but now Heidegger considers *Fundamental-ontologie* to be "the overcoming of metaphysics" (*Über-windung der Metaphysik*).[45] It is not a question here of simply putting in parentheses or of "reducing" metaphysics to reach its foundation, but of condemning the enterprise itself. *Überwinden,* which also means to conquer, betrays an intention that evidently has nothing to do with phenomenology at all. From the time of Plato, according to Heidegger, philosophy has lost its way by becoming metaphysics; it has lost and forgotten Being in order to attach itself to beings, because of its inability to distinguish them. "Now it is a question of clearing the way from metaphysics to the thought of the truth of Being."[46] "Metaphysics, inasmuch as it always represents being to itself merely as being, does not think Being itself. Philosophy does not commune with itself concerning its foundation. It abandons it, and this, because of metaphysics."[47] But by going back to the foundation of metaphysics, thought "will become truly thought."[48] The word of the poet will become "truly spoken."[49] In metaphysics rational and logical thought is a sort of dried fish; it is time to plunge thought back into Being which is its natural element.[50] "The thought that results is no longer philosophy because it thinks more originally than metaphysics." "Less philosophy and more respect for thought."[51] "Man ought, before speaking, once more let Being speak to him, at the risk of having little or nothing to say in answer to this call. Only thus is it possible to restore to the Word its essential value and to man the privilege of dwelling in the truth of Being."[52]

Consequently, if one wants to name, to speak, to think this radical foundation which is *Seyn* "without name," he has no other recourse than poetic or religious symbolism. This *trans-metaphysics* (that is the best name for it) expresses itself henceforth in images. This foundation will be a "dwelling," the "fatherland," the "home" to which, after forgetting Being, one returns.[53] For modern man is *heimatlos*,[54] "uprooted."[55] But he can find again, in the light of the *Da* where Being opens itself, the "nearness" to Being. "Man is the neighbor of Being."[56] "Man is not the lord of being, he is the shepherd of Being,"[57] and the poets and thinkers are the "guardians" of this dwelling-place.[58]

The image here is no longer a mere metaphor, an analogical footbridge to take us from the better known to the less known, from our familiar abodes to the Being-dwelling. The image has an ontological value; the day will come when, while really thinking Being, revealed at last in its (hitherto hidden) meaning of dwelling, we will understand in truth what "to dwell" means. It is as if the relationship of the symbol to what is symbolized were reversed. But here again we are frankly leaving phenomenology. Recourse to the image as the only means of expression is enough to show that. Phenomenology has no need of metaphors to operate the movement to the level of the foundation; the phenomenological reduction is sufficient. If we look carefully, we will see that Heidegger comes back, in a roundabout way and against his express intentions, to the classical conception of *metaphysical* ontology. For, if the foundation (Being) is not transcendental, and if the relation of Being to man is not established either on a single level (by reason for example) or by reduction, but only through the intermediary of a metaphorical language, then what could this foundation be except transcendent in a metaphysical sense?

Be that as it may, there is no longer a constituting consciousness and man does not construct Being by his thought. Properly speaking, it is not even man who thinks Being. Following the line of all his thought, Heidegger uses a more "neutral" formula: "the thought of Being comes to light in man."[59] For "man questions," he substitutes "it questions in man."[60] In this trans-metaphysics, which is a phenomenology in reverse, it is Being that makes man appear in revealing itself to him. In place of the phenomenological unveiling that brought out the intentional content of consciousness, Heidegger substitutes illumination or revelation pure and simple.[61] The hidden or the concealed that it is a question of disclosing is no longer the implicit or the latent as it was in Husserl, but the mysterious,[62] the sacred,[63] the numinous.

However, "Being is not God."[64] The traditional God is a "being." "Being is further away than any being and yet closer to man than any being, whether it be a rock, an animal, a work of art, a machine, whether it be an angel or

God."[65] Heidegger does not mean to declare himself "on the existence or non-existence of God—any more than on the possibility or non-possibility of the gods."[66] "Philosophy decides neither for nor against the existence of God. It remains indifferent."[67] How, in fact, could the philosopher whose mission is to think Being tarry over the paltry problem of the existence of a simple being, even if this being be God! Heidegger goes back beneath God, "he questions in a more radical manner." Like Germany's speculative mystics, he goes back from God to the "Divinity" (*die Gottheit*), from the Divinity to the "Sacred" (*das Heilige*), and from the Sacred to the Truth of Being.[68] By this radical going back to the foundation he naturally claims to go beyond the naive God of theism or of the faith of the common man. For him as for Hegel it is self-evident that "thought," philosophy, goes beyond and "comprehends" religion and faith. We enter a sort of speculative mysticism or negative theology, a tradition very much alive in German philosophy from the time of Eckhart, whom Heidegger calls "the ancient Master of doctrine and life,"[69] up to Hegel and Jaspers.

Such is the culmination of this philosophical "adventure" that leads to "the advent" or "the becoming" of Being.[70] Such is its style and aspect. Husserl wanted phenomenology to be sober and objective; it was to put human pathos in parentheses. Heidegger, by exacerbating this objectivism, has stripped Being of all that is human all too human, existent all too existent, but he has raised up around this Being, finally revealed in its distant proximity, a host of pathetic, poetic, and mystical overtones. Husserl tried to restore to an ever more lucid and reflexive consciousness a fullness of meaning which was rationality itself. Heidegger plunges us back into the fullness of a mystical nothingness, but the rationality of this Being-meaning has been sacrificed to a "thought" which wants to be more radical and more "thinking" than reason. Whether you still call this *philosophy* or not is of little importance, provided you know what you are saying, where you are going, and by what obscure lights the *Lichtung des Seins* illuminates you.

III THE PHENOMENOLOGY OF SARTRE

1. From Phenomenology to Existentialism

In our treatment of Heidegger we have shown the evolution "from phenomenology to ontology." It is necessary now to grasp the passage of phenomenology to what is designated by the ambiguous name of existentialism. In this way we take in the whole French phenomenological movement from the *Transcendence of the Ego* of Sartre to the *Phenomenology of Perception* of Merleau-Ponty.

At its origin phenomenology was a philosophy of essences, an "essentialism" rather than an existentialism. Putting any position regarding existence and all factual data in parentheses, it isolated ideal essences. Such was its point of departure, but we have already noted that Husserl ultimately arrived at the consecration of the lived world and that the insertion of consciousness in the world appeared more and more indestructible. This is the factual rooting in our lived existence that transcendental phenomenology disclosed ever more clearly. The "return to the things themselves" demonstrated very well that phenomenology remained faithful to the concrete and to existence, that it was, in short, an anti-idealism. To the extent that the reduction permits the intentionality of consciousness to appear, and that intentionality itself attaches consciousness to things and to the world, the existentialist "being-in-the-world" is already implicitly contained in the phenomenological method.[71] This very general remark already allows us to conceive the possibility of a continual progression from Husserl through Heidegger to Sartre.

But let us look concretely at the precise points where Sartre extends the thought of his predecessors and turns phenomenology in some new directions. On the appearance of *Being and Nothingness* some readers, struck by the presence of the major themes of Heidegger's thought, believed that Sartre had limited himself to "translating" or paraphrasing *Sein und Zeit*. In fact, it suffices to read Sartre with just a little attention to see a completely different orientation and especially to realize that Sartre is more Husserlian than Heideggerian (which is just the opposite of Merleau-Ponty).

Sartre so completely espoused the movement of Husserl's thought (unceasing search for an ever more radical foundation) that, like Heidegger, he was led from the first to radicalize again Husserl's program. Heidegger did it by turning to ontology and by abandoning the still too idealistic notion of transcendental consciousness to substitute for it a more ontological structure, the Dasein, which was a sort of fore-court of Being. It is also striking that the first thing Sartre did was to attack this transcendental Ego, but in order to radicalize it in an exactly opposite direction, to accentuate even more its character of consciousness and, in so doing, to bring out not being but existence. Sartre, in contrast to Heidegger, places himself at the heart of the phenomenological reduction. This latter, in Husserl, served to distinguish, at the borders of the world, a transcendental I which intended it and constituted it in its meaning as world. This Ego was a sort of transcendental "field" and could be described as a personal I, transcendental principle of unification, constitution, and meaning. In other words, only the psychological ego fell before the reduction, for the sake of a transcendental ego which, as successive reductions took place, appeared more and more clearly as the source of meaning and of the intentionality of consciousness towards the world. Sartre, on the contrary, thinks that, since in phenomenology consciousness is defined by intentionality, the addition of a transcendental I is superfluous and "renders the unifying and individualizing role of the I completely useless" and even "harmful."[72] "The transcendental I is the death of consciousness."[73] In order to disclose consciousness, it is necessary to proceed to the radical reduction not only of the world, but also of the Ego itself; that is to say, it is necessary to place the I on the side of the world, because the I is an object of consciousness just like all the other objects.

This amounts to ejecting *really everything* from consciousness. In consequence, the famous formula of intentionality, "all consciousness is *consciousness of* something," will take on an even more radical sense than before. There is not the least *content* of consciousness; there is not the slightest interiority, not even of an Ego or of a transcendental consciousness; everything is exterior to it. Consciousness radically expels all being outside itself, including the I; or rather, in the radical reduction, it takes its distance in relation to the whole of being. "The cogito asserts too much";[74] it is "impure." In fact the I is in the world and we should not say more than: "there is consciousness."[75] Sartre explodes the ego.[76]

This radical reduction which is of pure Husserlian inspiration and which constitutes the key to Sartre's thought, entails a series of quite fundamental consequences which reveal his originality in relation to Husserl as well as to Heidegger. Roughly speaking, we can say that Heidegger rejected the transcendental Ego-consciousness of Husserl for the sake of the Dasein, while, against Husserl, Sartre throws out the Ego the better to save the Husserlian consciousness against Heidegger,[77] and to rediscover, against Husserl but while remaining profoundly faithful to his intention, a purer notion of phenomenological consciousness. Let us then examine more closely the characteristics of this Sartrian consciousness.

1. If *everything* is exterior to consciousness, *consciousness is not anything, it is nothingness*. It is more bare than a tabula rasa.[78] The phenomenological reduction henceforth deserves to be baptized "nihilation." Consciousness, by nihilation, tears itself away from the world in a single jerk. There is no further need of those eternal repetitions, those unending approximations which characterize Husserl's approach. On the one side there is being, the fullness which is everything (being-in-itself); on the other is consciousness which breaks itself away from being, which becomes unstuck, which is nothingness or "being-for-itself." Of course this nothingness is not the *metaphysical* nonbeing of Parmenides, not an absolute nothingness; it is a transcendental or phenomenological nothingness, which is defined not in itself but in its relationship with being, characterized by the reduction which detaches it from and the intentionality which inserts it in being (withdrawal and intentionality being the obverse and reverse sides of nihilation).

Thus, in contrast to Husserl and Heidegger, ontology is not the always envisaged but never attained end of the phenomenological approach. In Sartre, as a result of radical nihilation, the dichotomy of being-in-itself and being-for-itself (or nothingness) is, so to speak, immediate. The "phenomenological ontology" of *Being and Nothingness* is not a method of progressive movement towards being; it is ontology *as* phenomenology. But by thus attaining its goal at a single stroke, the phenomenological method in Sartre is weakened as method. This gives Sartre's ontology a dogmatic, not to say a scholastic, look from the beginning. The reduction in the form of nihilation is so radical that phenomenology is swept away at the same time. It is as if the method of reduction, at the moment at which it succeeded by nihilation in "decompressing" the in-itself in the for-itself, being in consciousness, congealed itself, by a reverse movement, as massive ontology.

2. *Consciousness is consciousness of self.* For Husserl, all consciousness was intentional and one attained transcendental consciousness to the extent that, by reflexion or a reversing of intentionality, one went back from the psychological ego to the original Ego. For Sartre, the reduction is not reflexion but nihilation, and it leads consequently to a non-reflexive consciousness. Taken in itself consciousness is pure consciousness of itself, but "non-positional," without division: a consciousness (of) self, as Sartre writes it, or a self-consciousness, in short an implicit knowing of self.[79] The manner of existence of consciousness is to be consciousness of self.[80] Sartre separates himself from Husserl because he admits a dimension of consciousness other than intentionality ("positional of objects"). Traditional philosophy and psychology believed that this other dimension was of the reflexive order and that it was an interiority. Sartre opposes at once the intentional unidimensionality of Husserlian consciousness and the interiority of the reflexive philosophies proper to the French tradition (from Descartes to Maine de Biran, Bergson, and Lavelle). For him reflexion is not a means for discovering

original consciousness or absolute consciousness; it is necessary to understand reflexion on the basis of the nonreflexive or non-positional consciousness obtained by the method of reduction. Hence, a completely new theory of reflexion into which we cannot enter here. Sartre has outlined it in his distinction between "pure reflexion" and "impure reflexion."[81]

3. *Consciousness is existence without essence.* By means of the reduction of all being which is nihilation, consciousness emerges without any content, without the least interiority; it has no essence any more; it is no longer an essence in any sense, but pure spontaneity, pure existence. It is "complete lightness, complete translucency,"[82] "consciousness through and through,"[83] "absolute existent by dint of non-existence."[84] "All conscious existence exists as consciousness of existing"; "consciousness is a fullness of existence," an "absolute of existence."[85] In other words, its essence is henceforth what its intentionality intends; consciousness is no longer essence but project of essence. It is not what it is, that is why it is nothingness of essence; but it is what it is not, that is, of which it is the project. Now we comprehend the scope of Sartre's slogan: "Existence (of consciousness) precedes essence." Essence is always *in front of* us, "transcendent." It is never that on which our existence is based. The relationship of essence and existence is reversed; existence is no longer the "complement" of essence (*complementum possibilitatis*); it appears henceforth as the transcendental condition of the possibility of essence. The primacy of existence over knowledge also becomes clear, because the whole enterprise of knowledge is rooted in this consciousness which is pure existence.

Existence does not have here its classical meaning:[86] the actualization of a being, the reality of a being as opposed to its simple logical possibility, the fact of existing (on the contrary existence is "nothingness!"). Nor does it have the "existential" meaning of lived existence, nor the Kierkegaardian meaning of separation, of interiority or relation to transcendence, but rather a properly phenomenological meaning: existence designates the spontaneity *of consciousness* in the nihilating reduction. Existence is nothing other than consciousness. It is necessary to note the paradoxical fact that in his phenomenological philosophy Sartre offers us a conception of existence that is, strictly speaking, not in the least "existentialist"! Furthermore, in all his properly philosophical books and articles, from the *Transcendence of the Ego* to *Being and Nothingness,* the term existentialism never appears and the accent is never placed on the philosophy of existence. It was not until after his journalistic polemics of 1944–1946 that the term appeared under the pen of Sartre.[87] If it were a matter here of characterizing Sartre's existentialism as such, we would have to go to his literary works and we would have to make a very necessary distinction between inauthentic, absurd, viscous, and nauseous existence,[88] which is a lived and "existentiel" existence, and authentic, hard, virile existence, the existence of the "dry consciousness,"[89] that of the free man (that of Orestes in *The Flies* for example), which is ultimately nothing other than existence in the phenomenological sense: consciousness.

4. *Consciousness is freedom.* In tearing itself away from being in order to transform it into project, in liberating itself from its essence in order to direct itself completely on the basis of its existence towards what it proposes to be, consciousness arises as the source of its intention. This tearing-away is a rupture with all the determinations which would make of it an object among objects, a being, an in-

itself. This project is "recovered" on the basis of this pure existence; it is therefore pure spontaneity to the precise extent that consciousness is its own foundation. If the world and being as a whole are reduced, this means that they have become wholly intentional for consciousness. It is no longer possible to speak of the determination of consciousness by the world or by the in-itself, because for consciousness to arise means to arise free and to intend a world whose whole signification henceforth has its foundation in consciousness.

But, correlatively, this freedom, since it is not something, is wholly project, intentional of the world.[90] The autonomy of consciousness is not an acosmic freedom, without a world. The reduction nihilates the world; it does not annihilate it. It does not suppress being in itself; it makes it possible to recapture it differently. It does not detach consciousness; it engages it by bringing it to be consciousness *of world,* consciousness of situation. The phenomenology of Sartre, by radically reducing the world and even the Ego, forbids itself "to withdraw a particle of man outside the world,"[91] a particle which would be, for example, the free ego, for the ego is in the world, determined. And freedom (which, like nothingness, is transcendental) is relation of consciousness to the world, and not of the ego to the world. Freedom is not a new essence or a new qualification of consciousness; it is wholly "project" of a world. Sartre does not educe a sort of freedom essential to consciousness or to man, a paradisiacal freedom which he would then try to jam into the world and into action. There is no freedom that is not engaged, in situation; this is precisely "facticity." Thus we come to the best known themes of Sartre's philosophical and literary production. In view of the numerous excellent books available on this subject, it is not the purpose of this study to give still another résumé of it. Our aim is limited to outlining the properly phenomenological aspect of his undertaking. But, as in our study on Heidegger, it remains to show its outcome.

2. The Transcending or Abandonment of Phenomenology: Freedom and Action

If consciousness is nothingness and project, it is itself nothing and everything lies in front of it. It can be founded on nothing; it is its own foundation to the extent that it disengages itself from everything that is and from everything that it is in order to recover it in an act of free spontaneity. Nothing is given except that from which it is necessary to tear itself away. Consciousness is never given and human freedom, this agonizing and total freedom, if it is ontological or transcendental, is never an empirical datum at the point of departure. It is, on the contrary, the result of a radical phenomenological reduction. The point of departure is rather the "enmired freedom,"[92] the stuck or ensnared existence of *Nausea.*

Freedom is essentially project, that is to say task, project *of freeing itself;* it is discovered in action and is identical to it. Sartrian consciousness, instead of *being* (it has no essence), has to *make itself,* create itself, and since it is pure spontaneity, to choose itself and invent itself. And here Sartre's ontology is no longer based solely on the dichotomy of the in-itself and the for-itself. We see now that *being* is only a foil and that *doing* is at least equally important. "Having, doing and being are the cardinal categories of human reality."[93] For the first time phenomenology develops in the direction of a philosophy of doing, of creation, of action, in short of a "pragmatism" in the broad sense.[94] To be is to act. A truce to the traditional quarrels about *operari sequitur esse* or *esse sequitur operari*. Henceforth *operari = esse*.

But to make oneself is "to make oneself other," it is to transform. The nihilating withdrawal of consciousness is not a flight into the contemplative attitude or that of the "disinterested spectator" of Husserl; it is project of recovering and transforming. In Husserl the reduction was the *transformation of intentionality;* in Sartre nihilation is the *intention of transforming* the world (or the intention of *self*-transformation since the I is a part of the world). It sufficed, therefore, to push the phenomenological reduction to the limit, to reduce even the Ego and to arrive at a transcendental nothing-consciousness, in order for the intuitive, contemplative, disclosing philosophy that is phenomenology to transform itself into a philosophy of action, into a "philosophy of work," into a "philosophy of revolution."[95] And reciprocally, in Sartre—and this is the originality of his philosophy of action—there is no action that is not disclosure. It is precisely only action which enables us to see, to know. The nihilating withdrawal is a way of becoming unstuck from a situation in order to see it, to understand it, to transform it. All of which comes to one thing: comprehension and action go together.[96]

We also rediscover here the teleology, the finality so important in phenomenology. Consciousness is project: it throws itself ahead of itself into the future; one can understand what it is only by what it will be.[97] The phenomenological reduction signifies for Sartre that man tears himself away from his past and from determinism (from efficient causality, which goes from the past to the present), and projects himself out towards his future. "Try to grasp your consciousness and probe it; you will see that it is hollow;

you will find there only the future."[98] But the project is at the same time movement from the future towards the present (final causality). "Man is the being who comes to himself on the basis of the future,"[99] who "defines himself by his goals."[100] The goals which I propose to myself or which I project revert backwards to my present situation to clarify and transform it. And if there can be consciousness of the present, it is because of the distance which separates me from it, which is precisely the dimension of my project towards the future. The phenomenological reduction thus operated is then indeed freedom: a tearing-away from the determinism of the past and a returning from the future. We recognize the two complementary phenomenological movements: putting in parentheses (of the past) and intentionality, and the definition of consciousness of the present by this double movement.

But in this perspective of a philosophy of action, it is the present (and not the future as in Heidegger) that is ultimately most accentuated.[101] Sartre's teleology here differs from Husserl's. Originally phenomenology, by its method of disclosing, meant to bring out the hidden *meaning,* in the double sense of signification and of finality. This is to say that the end *was already there* in a latent form. Thus, the infinite task of philosophy was that of becoming conscious of what was not yet given but was already present in a certain manner: phenomenology presented itself as a consecration of the already there, as respect for the real.[102]

For Sartre, who seems here to have profited from the Bergsonian critique of finality, there is no already-there, because reduction goes as far as "nothingness." Intention aims at the *not-yet,* that which is not; not that which is latent but that which is future. This is why the consciousness-project will be able to reveal values only by creating them. There will be no given or latent values, because value never *is*. Man will only be what he actually makes himself; he will be the creator of values and the transformer of the real.

Nevertheless, since freedom is not a given but a project of liberation, it encounters resistance: not only the limits of a factual situation (facticity) with its menace of entrapment, but also the temptations of "bad faith" which incite us to shirk the responsibility and solitude of free decision. Since all action is transformation, effort, struggle, it comes up against *adversity* and it is *failure*. The theme of failure takes on a growing importance in Sartre.[103] Free consciousness is continually enmeshed in the stickiness from which it is unsticking itself. Its very success is its failure, for "success comprises a secret failure."[104] "By killing I *gave* myself *a nature. Before,* I dreamt of proving by my crime that I was escaping from all essence; *afterwards,* my essence is my crime, it strangles me in its iron fist."[105] In short, phenomenological reduction, described in the abstract, is performed in an instant. But, interpreted now as free action in the world and society or as liberation, it proves impossible of complete realization or at least it needs to be continually done over. It is here that Sartre's ethics is rooted, the ethics which he announced at the end of *Being and Nothingness*. "Thus any ethics which does not present itself explicitly as *impossible today* contributes to the mystification and alienation of men. The moral "problem" arises from the fact that ethics is *for us* both inevitable and impossible. Action must prescribe its ethical norms within this climate of insurmountable impossibility."[106] The circle which began from Husserl is closed here; Sartre's phenomenological ethics seems to present anew the appearance of the Husserlian method: eternal repetition, infinite and never achieved task. But if the infinite task must mean failure, if such must be the last word of this ethics, the Hydra of Lerna or the rock of Sisyphus emerges on the horizon and Husserl would no longer recognize himself in this distant progeny.

3. Humanism and Atheism

Sartre thus intends to base his conception of man on a new relationship between consciousness and the world, or rather on the double movement of tearing-away from the world (by nihilation) and the project of transforming engagement in this world. In tearing itself away from the world, consciousness casts outside itself not only things and the world, but everything in it which is still an object in any sense, all that *is,* every essence and every nature. The phenomenological reduction culminates in *the most radically anti-naturalistic conception of man* (and naturally also in the most anti-materialistic). Man is not an "animal," not even a reasonable one; he is not to be explained on the basis of the world and the other "kingdoms." Consciousness, emptied of the world (let us say rather "nothingness" since "emptied" would still suppose some interiority of consciousness conceived as a kind of recipient), pure existence without essence, pure subjectivity (not in the sense of subjectivism of course), holds up our humanity all alone. It is by it alone that we are men, as for Descartes.

But, in opposition to Descartes, this consciousness is not distinct from the world; it is wholly intention of the world from which it tears itself away. Its very nothingness weds it entirely to the world; and this intentionality defines it as specifically as does its nothingness or its freedom. It is in no sense an *object,* but wholly *project.* This is to say that man will not be defined by characteristics or a nature that

would be inherent in him, but solely by his worldly ven-
tures, by his acts.

Thus, if man is not an animal, he will not be explained,
either, in relation to God. If Sartre tears man away from
nature, it is not to throw him into the arms of God. Anti-
naturalism and the denial of interiority equally imply
atheism. In fact, if everything is really outside of consciousness, if consciousness has no interiority, we will not find in
it, in I know not what deep recess (consciousness is complete translucency!) an *intimior intimo meo,* a depth that
leads to something beyond man, a transcendence. Man is
defined without God. Sartre has wholly reduced the Ego
and the world. He proceeds likewise, one can say, to a
phenomenological reduction of God. As long as it is a question of discovering the humanity of man, consciousness
must tear itself away from God, as it tore itself away from
"its" Ego or from the world. Now, we have seen that what
the reduction puts in parentheses, consciousness conserves
or discovers as intentionality. God, therefore, is no longer
the foundation of man, but he subsists integrally as the intention[107] of man.

This atheism is a hundred leagues from the atheism of
the late nineteenth century. In fact, just as, for phenomenology, the problem of the *reality* of the external world no
longer has any meaning and is no longer posed, so in the
same way there is no longer any problem of the *existence*
of God.[108] "Existentialism is not an atheism in the sense
that it would wear itself out in trying to demonstrate that
God does not exist. It declares rather: Even if God existed,
that would change nothing."[109] The two central themes of
this atheism are the following:

1. The theme of *the absence of God,* as soon as it is a
matter of defining man, freedom, humanism. God is put in
parentheses and Sartre speaks of the "death of God" on the

authority of Nietzsche and by interpreting this death not in the sense of a murder committed by man (as was the case in Nietzsche), but in the sense of absence. "God is dead. Let us not understand by that that he does not exist or even that he no longer exists. He is dead. He spoke to us and he is silent. We no longer have anything but his cadaver. Perhaps he slipped out of the world, somewhere else, like the soul of a dead man. Perhaps he was only a dream . . . God is dead, but man has not, for all that, become an atheist."[110]

2. The theme of the *fascinating presence of this same absent God,* as soon as it is a matter of characterizing intentionality or the undertakings of man and of proceeding to his "existential psychoanalysis." "Man is fundamentally the desire to be God."[111] God is *the* regard in person, "the quintessence of the other,"[112] "forgetfulness, repose."[113] "Man loses himself that God may be born . . . Man is a useless passion."[114]

Sartre's phenomenology accustomed us to the notion of a reality of nothingness. We will not be astonished, then, that this atheism, obsessed simultaneously with the presence and absence of God, arrives at a sort of negative theology and rejoins certain classic themes of mysticism: the night of unknowing, the coincidence of contraries, superessential nothingness, etc.[115] In this respect *The Devil and the Good Lord* is particularly significant. This play brings us to the frightening coincidence of the presence and absence of God, of Evil and Good; of Evil for the sake of Evil and Good for the sake of Good, of faith and "bad faith," of blasphemy and witness, in short of the Devil and the Good God. "Night is falling. At twilight one needs strong eyes to distinguish the Good God from the Devil."[116] All transcendental values (positive and negative) are annulled and leave Goetz facing the solitary decision which creates values. After having wanted to hide himself in the "dark night away from the sight of other beings," after having cried to God: "Say, the night, it's you isn't it? Night, the frightening absence of everything! For you are the one who is present in universal absence . . ."[117] Goetz assumes his responsibilities as a man, regains lucidity: "The silence, it is God. Absence is God. God is the solitude of men."[118] He discovers that he is a man; he rediscovers men. "I am beginning everything all over again."[119] "I want to be a man among men."[120]

Man finds his humanity at the moment when the double annulment of values, their double reduction, reveals the solitude of his consciousness. But God is not simply denied; rather, he is nihilated. He becomes a purely intentional God, "transcendent" in the phenomenological sense in which one speaks of the transcendence of the world or of the Ego in respect to consciousness. It is God for man, consciousness *of* God (God intended by consciousness) that the reduction of God discloses.[121] This phenomenological atheism, which has nothing in common with the indifferentism of Heidegger, is enriched by the Nietzschean theme of the "God is dead," but it is impoverished sometimes also by suddenly falling back to the level of popular atheism, to pure blasphemy or even to the "naughtiness"[122] which shows a good old stock of anti-clericalism rather than a new philosophical position on the problem of God.

Thus, even if we travel towards shores very different from the horizons of Husserl, the phenomenological method in Sartre does not seem to be totally extinguished as we had to note in the case of Heidegger. Sartre is far from having said his last word. His thought is oriented, like that of Merleau-Ponty, towards the analysis of engagement, action, and history.[123] The French phenomenologists, who are the philosophers of the "Resistance," brutally thrown into history and encamped before Marxism, cannot dodge these questions.

IV THE PHENOMENOLOGY OF MERLEAU-PONTY

1. *"Radical Reflexion" or the "Phenomenology of Phenomenology"*

Sartre pushed the radicalism of the phenomenological method in the direction of the tearing-away from the fullness, from massive and sticky being. The reduction proceeded to a decompression, to a nihilation which led to a naked and perfectly translucent consciousness. To be sure, Sartre did not deny or forget the world, but he did not think that it was possible to put it in parentheses or to recover it otherwise than from the standpoint of the transcendental nothingness of consciousness.

Merleau-Ponty conceives the radicalism of the reduction to lie in an exactly opposite movement. It is, for him, the means of becoming conscious of our indestructible relationship to the world, of revealing this world and its "inalienable presence."[124] "We never remain suspended in nothingness. We are always in the fullness, in being, like a face which, even when asleep, even when dead, is always condemned to express something . . . and like the silence which is still a modality of the world of sound" (p. 516). "We are relation to the world through and through" (p. viii) and "true philosophy is a re-learning to see the world" (p. xvi). By the reduction Merleau-Ponty does not understand a withdrawal from the world towards a pure consciousness. If he withdraws, if he "distends the intentional ties that bind us to the world," it is "precisely in order to see the world" (p. viii) and to become aware of our relationship to it.

Thus, it is impossible for us "to reduce ourselves to transcendental consciousness" and to "become wholly consciousness" (p. 76). All consciousness, all knowledge, all human undertakings are drawn on an ever present substratum: the world, a world that is always already-there, radically primary. The reduction will be neither an idealistic movement, a "return to a transcendental consciousness before which the world unfolds itself in an absolute transparence" (p. v), nor a reflexive return to an interior source, to "the interior man" of Saint Augustine, but "the formula of an existential philosophy," of a "subject wedded to the world" (pp. ix and v).

In spite of everything he owes to Sartre, Merleau-Ponty thus finds himself in opposition to him on the fundamental questions of consciousness and freedom. My existence is not reduced to the consciousness I have of existing, as for Sartre. "The idea of a consciousness that would be transparent to itself and whose existence would be reduced to the consciousness it has of existing is not very different from the notion of unconsciousness" (p. 436). In other words, in the *Cogito ergo sum,* it is not the "I think" that eminently contains the "I am"; it is consciousness which is reintegrated in existence (p. 439) or which grasps itself in a sort of ambiguity or obscurity that prevents it precisely from being pure consciousness or absolute existence (p. 432). "I am present to myself by being present to the world" (p. 466). "The *Cogito* must reveal me in situation" (p. vii), engaged in a total, equivocal historical situation. This existence will not be anxiety or "virile restlessness" as for Sartre, but *ambiguity,*[125] not damnation, but chance and risk.

Freedom, also, will no longer be that of Sartre, which

Merleau-Ponty has subjected to a penetrating criticism.[126] The perpetual tearing-away by which Sartre defined freedom appears to Merleau-Ponty only as "the negative aspect of our universal engagement in the world" (p. 501). "Far from my freedom being always alone, it is never without accomplice, and its power of perpetual tearing-away is based on my universal engagement in the world. My effective freedom is not on this side of my being, but in front of me, in things" (p. 516). Without these roots freedom would not be freedom, but in this rootedness is expressed the irreducible ambiguity of my existence, of my participation in the world (p. 520). "I am never a thing and never naked consciousness" (p. 517). The principal complaint that Merleau-Ponty thus makes against Sartre is, it seems, that nihilation, just like idealistic reflexion, "carries itself off and converts itself into an invulnerable subjectivity" (p. iv).

For Merleau-Ponty,[127] the phenomenological reduction on the contrary reveals the world, the world of perception (the perceived world), the natural and social world (p. 418), in short, the original world. And the more radical the reflexion is, the less the world appears transparent. That is to say, the more reflexion manifests "its dependence with respect to a non-reflexive life" (p. ix), the better we will realize that reflexion remains incomplete so long as it is not aware of its own beginning (p. iv). The phenomenological method furnishes the means of "reflecting on this reflexion" ("reflexion of the second degree," "radical reflexion"), by revealing that it is directed to something unreflected (pp. 75, 77, 253, 278), but that it tends precisely to reveal it *as unreflected* without reabsorbing it into an absolute consciousness. "Reflexion is really reflexion only if it is not carried outside itself, only if it knows itself as reflexion-on-the-unreflected, and consequently as a change of structure of our existence" (p. 76).

It is not possible for such a reflexive consciousness to "fly above" the world, and "there is no thought which embraces the whole of our thought" (p. ix). This radical philosophy "is a renewed experience of its own beginning, it consists wholly in describing this beginning" (p. ix). If reflexion becomes aware of an irreducible unreflected as its own substratum, it is necessary to understand this unreflected not as something that is *not yet* reflected (because still unconscious and offered to our reflexion), but as an unreflected that reflexion reveals as its own upholder and point of support, as its radical point of departure. This is the world or our original relationship to the world. The reduction[128] is the only form of reflexion that does not reabsorb the unreflected, but rather points it out. As we see, the position of Merleau-Ponty implies that consciousness is no longer primary, no matter how central it may be in phenomenology. "The true transcendental" is the world (p. 418), and not Being (as for Heidegger) nor consciousness (as for Sartre). The paradoxical and profound result is that what consciousness intends and recovers without ceasing is the world of which it is a part and out of which all its undertakings (and all reflexion) come forth. This is not what traditional philosophy calls the external world, the object of cosmology, but the existential relationship of man to the world.[129] In this way Merleau-Ponty makes the *being-in-the-world* of Heidegger (more original than consciousness) the true goal of the Husserlian reduction. He hopes thus to recover the profound unity of phenomenological and existential ambitions. The true transcendental or "existential" (to speak like Heidegger) is "the ambiguous life" (p. 418), for "we are mixed up with the world and with others in an inextricable confusion."[130]

In Merleau-Ponty, more than in any other phenomenologist, we observe that the putting in parentheses of the world operated by the reduction is in fact the unveiling and bringing into relief of this world as such. Phenomenological description revealed to us the "phenomenal" world; the phenomenological reduction of Merleau-Ponty gives us the world as transcendental: radical reflexion still remains a description, but as redoubled. "It is necessary that these descriptions be for us the occasion of defining an understanding and a reflexion that will be more radical than objective thought. To phenomenology, understood as direct description, must be added a phenomenology of phenomenology. We must return to the *cogito* to look there for a Logos more fundamental than that of objective thought, which gives the latter its relative rights and at the same time puts it in its place" (p. 419). By reflecting on the foundation of reflexion one arrives thus not at "a stratum of prelogical experiences" (p. 419), but at the "phenomenon of the phenomenon" (p. 77). This redoubling of reflexion shows that the "logical" or phenomenological approach is essentially a repetition and consequently that it is never complete. "It will thus repeat itself indefinitely; it will be, as Husserl says, an infinite dialogue or meditation, and in the very measure to which it remains faithful to its intention, it will never know where it is going. The incompleteness of phenomenology and its inchoative appearance are not the signs of failure; they are inevitable because the task of phenomenology is to reveal the mystery of the world and the mystery of reason" (p. xvi).

2. From "Perception" to Expression and to History[131]

If phenomenology is "an inventory of consciousness as the milieu of the universe,"[132] the whole question of the natural experience of the world must be taken up on a different basis from that provided by experimental psychology and traditional epistemology. This is the task of Merleau-Ponty's first two books: *The Structure of Behavior* and *The Phenomenology of Perception*. Based on the experimental results of Gestalt psychology and behaviorism (while criticizing the framework of their interpretations of the observed phenomena), Merleau-Ponty attempts to show that perception is our orginal relation to the world, "a type of originary experience."[133] "Thus we should not ask whether we really perceive a world; we should say on the contrary: the world is what we perceive."[134] The world of perception is discovered "as the cradle of significations, the meaning of all meanings, the ground of all thoughts."[135]

But "meaning" has a new sense for Merleau-Ponty: it is the ambiguous but fundamental Logos, already present in our original relation to the world. "There is meaning,"[136] not *a* meaning. Meaning is ambiguous, mixed up with non-meaning[137] because the reduction is never complete. One can no more say that everything has meaning than that everything is nonsense. But we take up this meaning, which is unreflected rationality, by reflexion; we prolong it, and each of our acts, each of our thoughts expresses or gives a meaning to the world, without ever expressing it completely. "The idea of a *complete* expression makes no sense."[138] The meaning is not already-there, as if we had only to decipher the world. Nor is it we who, on the basis of our naked consciousness, create meanings and values, but "we express in a precise word the confused discourse of the world."[139] The whole problem of language and aesthetics must be taken up again.[140] There Merleau-Ponty will show first of all the presence of meaning in signs, then the passage from the gestural meaning of words to conceptual meaning, from the speaking word to the spoken word:[141] there will be between the two the same relationship as between perception and scientific thought.

On the plane of action and history,[142] we rediscover the same ambiguity and the same dialectic of meaning and non-meaning. "There would be no history if everything had a meaning and if the evolution of the world were nothing but the visible realization of a rational plan; but there would not be history either . . . if everything were absurd, or if the course of things were dominated by a few massive and unchangeable facts."[143]

At each of these levels Merleau-Ponty refuses the temptation to fly above the world. We are in the world, "we are born into reason as into language,"[144] we swim in meaning, we are in history and in political action. "We are historical through and through."[145] Everywhere Merleau-Ponty points out "an inevitable ambiguity,"[146] not for the pleasure of denouncing, from the top of an ivory tower of purity, the impurity of "the evil" of political action, the nonsense of the world, the terror or the violence of history, but on the contrary to invite us to "join ourselves to history instead of contemplating it,"[147] to admit that we are "embarked in experience" and that philosophy is nothing else than "a more acute consciousness"[148] of this experience. Here Merleau-Ponty, like Sartre, defends a humanism: It is high time for us "to think as living beings."[149] "The human world is an open or unachieved system and the same fundamental contingency which threatens it with discord at the same time delivers it from the fatality of disorder and forbids us to despair of it."[150] "The hero of our contemporaries is not Lucifer, it is not even Prometheus, it is man."[151] "Only the hero lives with his whole strength his relation to men and the world."[152]

GENERAL CONCLUSION

We have taken the liberty of tracing a line across a half-century of phenomenology. We began with the first problem of Husserl and the method of reduction that he inaugurated, by trying to recapture the profound intention of his method and to follow the movement of radical reflexion which he launched, up to its principal present-day realizations. In an already overcrowded current, this cavalier view does not pretend in any way to be panoramic. We are not forgetting that there have been and will be other phenomenologists, other phenomenologies.

Can we nevertheless answer the original question: What is phenomenology? It is above all method—a method for changing our relation to the world, for becoming more acutely aware of it. But at the same time and by that very fact, it is already a certain attitude vis-à-vis the world, or more exactly a certain attitude vis-à-vis our relation to the world. Phenomenology combines the most radical break with our ordinary and natural attitude vis-à-vis the world (in this sense, it is an ascesis of the mind) with the deepening or the consecration of this original attitude (in this sense, it is respect for the real and engagement in the world). Consciousness takes its distance with regard to things; it gives itself complete freedom in respect to them, but one realizes at once that this is in order to be more faithful to our essential insertion in the world. The reduction of the world is, for consciousness, a circuitous way of assuming it more fully, of taking in tow the meaning of the world. It is in this that phenomenology is an adventure of consciousness much more than a system of the world or a *Weltanschauung*. But this does not detract in any way from the extreme objectivism of this philosophy, an objectivism that remains a constant throughout the course of this long

and multiple effort of going back "to the things themselves" and of restoring the most originary real in all its
meaning. The phenomenological method thus permits
pushing on simultaneously and with one movement towards the roots of subjectivity and the foundation of the
objective world.

It will have been remarked—and this is what renders a
characterization of the whole movement so difficult—that
this philosophical method is animated by a power of going-
beyond that is really disconcerting, and that, itself a perpetual repetition, it forces us to an incessant repetition of
what we believed was already acquired. This is as true of
the idea that we are trying to construct of phenomenology
as of the very object of its investigations. Phenomenology is
description, but it is more than that: it is radical searching
for foundations, transcendentalism. It presents itself as
method, and yet it implies a complete view of the world. It
is disclosure of phenomena, but at the same time it is a return to the self or to the subject. It aims at essences, and it
ends up in existence. It puts in parentheses the factual and
the psychological datum, and yet it finally restores the lived
world.

This going-beyond manifests itself in the passage to
ontology and existentialism which we have traced. On the
one side phenomenology shows itself capable of rediscover-
ing and renewing the traditional and fundamental problems of philosophy, those that the positivism and the epistemology of the nineteenth century lost sight of; for example, the problem of being, which phenomenology is able
to pose again in a new way and with metaphysical boldness.
By its radicalism it unites itself, against the closing nineteenth century, with the profound and integral intention
of the philosophy of all ages. But, on the other side, it rejoins by its own paths the quite recent current of existen-

tialism that comes from Kierkegaard and Gabriel Marcel, by infusing it with a new force and a new spirit, and by bringing to it a method of "rigorous science."

Even if we have not been able to describe in detail the fecundity of the phenomenological method in more diverse areas, nor completely unravel the skein of the multiple phenomenologies that exist, at least it appears clearly that in the course of this philosophical thrust the conception of the relationship of man to the world, of consciousness to being, and especially of the reflexive relationship of consciousness to itself, has been profoundly modified. It is evidently premature to answer the question that very naturally poses itself to us here: Is it here that the view of man and of the world that will be and will remain that of the twentieth century is being forged? It suffices for the moment to observe that, at the very least, phenomenology is and will remain one of those that counts today.

The Question of the Radical Point of Departure in Descartes and Husserl

I
T IS POSSIBLE to define philosophy as the search for what is first, for the *arché* (ἀρχή) or the *próton* (πρῶτον). Philosophy is essentially an "archology"[1] or "protology."[2] But the double sense of *arché* and of *próton* opens up a double perspective from the beginning.

The *arché* is either a non-temporal *próton*, whose priority is ontological or logical, i.e., a *principle*, or it is a temporal *próton* whose priority is chronological, i.e., a *beginning*. Philosophy will be considered either as *a science of principles, epistéme tôn próton archôn* (ἐπιστήμη τῶν πρώτων ἀρχῶν),[3] first philosophy, or as *a science of the beginning,*[4] concerned with the *arché philosophias* (ἀρχή φιλοσοφίας)[5] or with taking the first step, a science of procedure, a search for a method or a route, an "investigation of the first truth" (Lequier), a temporal dialectic.

In the first sense, the principle is the point of the original rooting of philosophy, its foundation and base; it is certitude and solution. To say *arché* is as much as to say a completed philosophy; nothing is left but to deduce or explicate: the die is cast.

In the second sense, the *arché* is an open question; it is the uneasiness of the philosopher who is anxious to take root in the truth, in an original truth; it is the anxiety of not missing the entrance, of finding his footing, like a

93

mountain-climber. Here it is a question of philosophy as something to be done, as a task and as a search.

When it is thus the original foothold of philosophical reflexion and not the principle of things which becomes the major preoccupation of the philosopher, there is a *primum* and a *deinde*. We are not on the same level as truth and the problem of the entrance and of the route is posed. Precisely because there is a step to take, and to take correctly, there is a problem of the beginning. The philosophical question of the beginning constitutes then the beginning of the question, of philosophical questioning.

But we are already confronted with doubt (*aporia*). If the point of departure is in question, are we not condemned never to start, but to mark time within the limits of a question which we can break out of only by an act of violence, by a gratuitous leap that would establish some place to begin? Or are we not forced to recognize that by posing this question we have in fact already started on our way and that the question as we have posed it no longer has any meaning: it has been decided. It can only be a matter of re-commencing. This would amount to saying that no beginning is possible, or that every beginning is necessarily an unfounded pre-sumption, a prejudice.

In reality, the question is neither annulled nor resolved; this is, as a matter of fact, the very meaning of the word *aporia*. The philosopher appears, by definition, to lack a starting point; either he cannot begin or he has already begun. Therefore, the beginning is a problem, not an insoluble problem or even a false problem, but a *radical* philosophical question in the proper sense of the term. The awareness of this situation of a problematic beginning is precisely philosophy become a radical question to itself. Its job is not only to discover the first principle of reality, but its own principle, the very foundation of its enterprise of reflexion and questioning. The question of the radical point of departure can only be the question of philosophy itself; it can only be radical reflexion, that is to say reflexion on the foundation of reflexion.

We observe from the start that the problem of the beginning, while remaining first in time, is not a simple preliminary problem or a problem of method. In fact, the chronological priority of the beginning and the ontological priority of the principle together constitute a single and identical question, and this is precisely what renders it radical. A first temporal act of reflexion should at the same time take on the character of the absolute evidence of a non-historical principle. For a radical philosophy there is no *first* which merits this title unless it unites in itself logical and chronological priority, unless it is the foundation and source of apodicticity. This is so true that it will be impossible to say whether it is the first principle that founds the initial act of reflexion, or whether it is the inaugural act which constitutes the principle; whether it is the method which leads to being or whether it is being which founds the method. A philosophy of the radical point of departure is a philosophy which, from its very roots, intimately fuses the first temporal act of reason with the non-temporal value of reason, which tends to unite the temporal and the logical, in other words which begins immediately with an absolute act, an act which contains the absolute or which involves an absolute in some way and by that very fact involves man as a whole in the reflexion which poses or discloses the first and apodictic principle.

We see in what sense we can speak of a radical beginning. It is not only, as in Hegel, because the dialectical step that uncovers the absolute constitutes the absolute; it is not only because there is no result which can be given independently of its discovery. We have not placed ourselves at

the level of the result but at the level of the point of departure, and that is where the absolute and apodicticity are
situated. The question of the beginning is inevitably expressed in terms of a radicalization of the philosophical
question, and even in terms of a radicalization of the problem of man. It is clear that the problem of the radical point
of departure is thinkable only in a philosophy of the reflexive type, that is to say in a philosophy in which man
himself and his quality of being a subject are truly at stake
in the philosophical question. If man is placed radically in
question, if he reflects radically on himself, he will have to
answer this question; he will have to grasp himself by an
absolute and initial act that will be an act-principle.

All philosophical radicalism implies by that very fact
the will and the responsibility of man at the heart of the
absolute principle that he poses and of the apodictic evidence that he is looking for. From the start it goes beyond
epistemology, the level of critical judgment, and aims at
fusing together the moral will and the grasping of evidence, the ethical and the metaphysical. It is the will which
wills the beginning and which untiringly brings reflexion
back to it. The radical is voluntary in the sense that it is always necessary to will in order to begin. Every beginning
is against nature; the beginning is a leap and nature does
not make leaps. Nature draws you away from the beginning and urges you to persevere in your being. The beginning can be taken only with effort, regained only by going
against the current. Awaking is always an uprooting, a
sort of *fiat* that implies a renunciation and an ascesis. It is
the first step that costs and that counts for him who wills
to philosophize radically and become "a true beginner."[6]

But of course there are many ways to philosophize radically. Think of Protagoras or Socrates, of the Skeptics or
Descartes, of Fichte or Hegel, of Kierkegaard or Lequier, of

Nietzsche, of Bergson or Husserl. The following exposition is limited to the confrontation of Husserlian and Cartesian radicalism. Husserl placed himself consciously in the tradition of Descartes and even claimed that transcendental phenomenology was the fulfillment of Cartesian radicalism. Our task will be to clarify these two radicalisms, one by means of the other, and to examine the reproach which Husserl addresses to Descartes, namely that he misunderstood the scope of his discovery (transcendental subjectivity) and that he did not remain faithful to his radicalizing intention.

1. THE INTENTION OF RADICALISM

Descartes and Husserl share the common conviction that the task of philosophy is to establish the radical and apodictic foundation of the true science, the *mathesis universalis*. But the historical context is so different that this common search and this common preoccupation are oriented very differently. In fact, Descartes opposed Scholasticism and late Renaissance philosophy, while Husserl opposed relativistic and psychologistic positivism, and the neo-kantianism of the end of the nineteenth century.

The intention of philosophical radicalism itself is not identical in these two philosophies because the crisis of science, the crisis of the foundations which is its source, does not have the same significance. Descartes defined his ambition in reference to an uncertain science and philosophy, and his reform aimed initially at making a clean slate, then at remaking science *ab ovo*. It was a question of assuring the basis of an unshakeable certitude, of a cornerstone for the edifice of future science. His radicalism consisted in taking himself back, so to speak, this side of the *first*, in beginning again from zero and in discovering the true I, the first truth.

Husserl, on the other hand, found himself in the presence of a secure science, a completed science, in possession of its practical usefulness and its uncontested results. It was the same situation as that of Kant in face of Newton. The crisis of science did not touch its results but only its foundations and its meaning. This is evident at each step in Husserl's evolution: it is the problem of a pure logic in the *Logische Untersuchungen*, then the Kantian problem par excellence of the *Triftigkeit* in the *Idee der Phänomenologie* (how are the objective judgments which exist in fact possible?), finally the problem of the meaning of science in the *Krisis*.

When it is a question of establishing the foundations of a science yet to come, one turns towards metaphysics, but when it is a question of discovering foundations of a science already completed (and which was developed in the course of centuries in opposition to metaphysics, by the progressive and radical elimination of any metaphysical presupposition), one can only reflect on the knowledge that is already there. One starts reflexion at the level of logic or epistemology with an attitude of metaphysical neutrality, if not with a positively anti-metaphysical postulate. And if one does not want to fall immediately into a facile relativism or empiricism, it is necessary to turn, like Kant and ultimately Husserl, towards a transcendental investigation. For Husserl, the aim of radicalism does not consist in bringing himself back, by means of the doubt, this side of knowledge and in starting over again from nothing. It consists rather in grasping again more originally, on a new (transcendental) level, what is and always will be already there.

Under these circumstances the meaning of the expression or the content of the notion of a radical point of departure, as well as the method of radicalization, as we shall see, cannot be identical.

2. THE PROCESS OF RADICALIZATION

The enterprise of radicalization comes up against numerous obstacles; the terrain is obstructed. The suspension by *epoché* (ἐποχή), a sort of intellectual ascesis, will enable us to bring it out.

In Descartes the mind is encumbered by a doubtful science, by the multiplication of prejudices. These are swept away by means of the suspension of judgment and the methodic doubt which eliminates the uncertain, the pre-reflexive. The first foundation is established against the previous reality, in its place, by elimination.

In Husserl the terrain is occupied by a science that is certain, by facts and objective results, by all this *Reales* that monopolizes our view. There is nothing to eliminate, it is only necessary to free our view, to disengage the intuition of essences and foundations from it. But these foundations will be the foundations of the real that is already there and that remains there. The phenomenological reduction cannot be anything other than a change of perspective, of intuition and of intentionality. It tends, if one can say so, to immobilize a scene under an absent look in order to enable the eye to turn itself towards what renders this scene possible and gives it its meaning. It is understood that the *epoché* is from the beginning an enterprise of transcendental constitution and by that very fact the consecration of the pre-reflexive world.

In both cases, however, radicalization takes the form, at first sight identical, of a *fight against the evident*. For these two philosophers of intuition, haunted by the obvious, evidence is both the downfall and the salvation of consciousness. The struggle is necessary because evidence is not, unfortunately, immediately equivalent to apodicticity. It is necessary to detach oneself from evidences which are too obvious in order to grasp again a new evidence of radical beginning. The first move is thus an act of defiance with regard to the all too present evidence which alienates consciousness and hides reason from itself. Thus we use rational and scientific evidence to get rid of a first layer of naive evidences; then in a decisive radicalization we place these two kinds of evidence together under the test of a new *epoché*. This is the violent phase of the *epoché*, "hyperbolic" in Descartes, "against nature" in Husserl, which should clear away at the very heart of the evidence a more profound layer of naiveté, unmask the evidence as such, in order to bring out the apodictic evidence and open up access to the radical point of departure.

By using the indications of Husserl, we could say that the process of radicalization carries us from the obvious to an understanding of self, from the *Selbstverständlichkeit*[7] or false evidence to the *Selbstverständigung*[8] or to the *Selbstverständnis*,[9] that is to say to the Ego, radical foundation and new evidence, apodictic evidence.

But under the apparent similarity of this approach and of this second and radical *epoché* lie hidden profound and decisive radicalizing experiences as opposed as it is possible to imagine: the strictly metaphysical experience of the evil genius in Descartes, the experience of the transcendental reduction in Husserl.

In fact, the intervention of the evil genius, a decisive moment of the Cartesian *epoché* (which Husserl totally ignores even though he appeals to Descartes), is a methodological stratagem of metaphysical radicalization.[10] Thanks to it, Descartes, by a kind of assault against the still too naive evidence (even rational evidence), brings out the radical evidence of the foundation and finally discovers his point of departure. In the first stage of doubt Descartes feigned sleep in order to neutralize the illusory evidence of dreaming and, thanks to this stratagem, he perceived that the rational evidence of $2 + 3 = 5$ resisted the apparently irreducible opposition of wakefulness and sleep and permitted him to overcome it: "Whether I am awake or asleep, two and three added together will always make five."[11] In the second step of doubt, the step of hyperbolic and properly metaphysical radicalization, we find the same approach and the same feint on a new level. Descartes pretends to be deceived by someone stronger than he; he takes in hand the manipulation of the illusion in order to get out of it (this is what he calls to deceive oneself[12]); he has recourse to the feigned illusion of the evil genius in order to unmask the evidence, this time to neutralize the illusion of rational evidence itself. And behold, thanks to this stratagem, a radical and metaphysical evidence, that of the *sum*, resists the apparently irreducible and decisive opposition between being deceived and not being deceived: "There is no doubt that if he is deceiving me, I am; and let him deceive me as much as he will, he will never make me to be nothing as long as I think I am something."[13] "It seems to me that I am" is in fact equivalent to "I am." I am conscious of being, therefore I am. I think [myself] to be, therefore I am.[14] As opposed to illusory sensible evidence and even to rational mathematical evidence, this apodictic evidence is radical in the sense that it does not alienate the ego who says *sum*, because it is consciousness of itself, consciousness of being. It assures the ego of its first immediate and absolute hold in being. The constraining power of the evidence *sum* no longer alienates me, no longer creates a screen between myself and myself, for the artifice of the evil genius eliminates all alienation from the ego by showing that the fascinating gulf which continually threatened to plunge me back into illusion or nothingness, the gulf between "I imagine that I am" and "I am," is quite simply non-existent.

The Husserlian *epoché* answers an entirely different preoccupation. It is not an artifice to eliminate illusion and error and to insert us in being, but a means of neutralizing our natural belief in the world (whose *Selbstverständlichkeit,* however, is not at all illusory as such) and a mode of transcendental reflexion that aims at enabling us to take our distance with respect to being. This elimination does not concern my relationship to myself as in Descartes, but my relationship to the world. Far from isolating the ego by tearing it out of the world, far from leading to a pure residual consciousness, it modifies our relation to the world. It engages us differently, more profoundly, with respect to the world. It opens up a new domain of experience (the transcendental), it simultaneously discloses the transcendental subject (as condition for the meaning of the world, as constituting the meaning of the world, and intending the unity of its meaning)—and this meaning itself.

The grasping of self outside the world by reduction is a more explicit coming to awareness of the world as it is related to a consciousness. It is, therefore, much less a "reduction" of the ego by an elimination of the sensible or the empirical, much less a reduction to a transcendental nucleus of apodicticity, than a modification of the ego and of its attitude in relation to the world. It is a change of intentionality. One can scarcely speak of an awareness of self in this *Selbstbesinnung* because it is basically a question of a recovery of the world. Transcendental intentionality is attention to the world; what is uncovered is the relation of the world to its transcendental source which gives it meaning, and this is the new evidence. From being *latent,* consciousness of the world and of its meaning becomes *patent,*[15] while for Descartes consciousness as consciousness of the world is confused and becomes distinct by attending to itself.

These two experiences betray the fundamental opposition between two conceptions of consciousness. Let us not forget that the first result of the radicalizing *epoché* is to reveal the intimate structure of the consciousness that accomplishes it. It is in this sense that it is a return to self, *Selbstbesinnung,* a movement towards consciousness of self and the understanding of self.

In Descartes the *epoché* thwarts the natural dispersion of consciousness which tends to drown itself in confusion, for the world is the diversion of consciousness. If Descartes closes his eyes and ears, if he extinguishes his senses and cuts off his contact with the world, it is in order to render the interiorization or the meditative self-communion of consciousness possible, this concentration which is *attention.* By contracting itself, consciousness intensifies itself and thus becomes capable of *distinguishing* what had been confused. It grasps itself again in its essential structure which is attention, by making the world disappear.[16]

Husserl's *epoché,* on the contrary, makes the world (the sense of the world) appear and discloses the essential structure of phenomenological consciousness which is *intention.* The reduction modifies this intentionality: instead of losing itself in the world which it experiences, consciousness *discloses* it by grasping itself again as intention, that is to say as consciousness of meaning.

The place of radical apodicticity for Descartes is the attentive and intensified *I*, grasping itself as *sum* and managing to distinguish what was as yet confused. In Husserl it is the transcendental and intentional I (entirely consciousness of . . .), intending the world and managing to disclose what was as yet hidden or latent. Thus we see that the radical point of departure for Descartes lies at the very center of the concentrated and centripetal consciousness, and for Husserl at the terminal point of its centrifugal intention.

In both cases the process of radicalization is a reflexive procedure; it is a meditation or *Selbstbesinnung*. But, if it is a question of an attentive consciousness, reflexion tends to guarantee an Archimedian point, a hold. If it is a question of an intentional consciousness, it is *Be-sinnung*, a way of giving a *Sinn*, a sense, that is to say of disclosing at once a finality and a meaning. Consciousness of self frees Descartes from the weight of prejudices, from the whole badly digested store of experience, and it guarantees a new hold in being and opens up the future to him. Husserl conceives the *Selbstbesinnung* as a return, a re-grasping which should give a meaning to what we have experienced and thought.

Thus we find in Descartes the virginal beginning and the linear method, going forward without returning or recovery, following the order of reasons which are irreversible. While in Husserl we see a circular movement which revolves around its point of departure, radicalizes it progressively without ever truly leaving it. This movement, by displaying itself simultaneously as reduction and intentionality, digs ever deeper, and in its exhausting "struggle for the beginning,"[17] for a beginning which is an end "situated at infinity,"[18] is consumed by a coming and going which Husserl himself characterized as zig-zag.[19]

3. THE RADICAL POINT OF DEPARTURE

The reflexive return to self, in the process of radicalization, orients us according to Descartes towards the *awareness of self* (taking consciousness of self), and according to Husserl towards the *awareness of the world*. To the extent that this process is realized, we can say that attention accomplishes the coincidence of consciousness with itself, and intention, the coincidence of consciousness with the world. What remains is to show specifically that it is in these two types of coincidence that the difference between the two radical points of departure lies.

First we must note, once again, a fundamental divergence in the manner of conceiving the structure of consciousness. For Descartes, a thought is not only consciousness of its object, but always at the same time consciousness of itself, consciousness of the act of thought in the process of being realized. In the *Réponses aux Quatrièmes Objections* he writes in fact: "It is impossible for us to have within us any thought, without having actual knowledge of it at the very moment it is in us." To say it in the language of Sartre, all positional consciousness of objects is accompanied by a non-positional consciousness of self. Or to speak the language of Franz Brentano, which is also that of Aristotle: in every psychic phenomenon, besides the primarily intended object there is always *en parego* (ἐν παρέγῳ), like a second object, consciousness of self. It is in this second accessory, psychological consciousness that there is realized, without any reflexive doubling, a coincidence of the ego with itself. This coincidence is given at the start, but attention neglects it, passes over it to concentrate on the object. But this very real embryonic coincidence can become distinct consciousness of self whenever the attention or the contention is directed on it to intensify it. The

Cartesian *cogito* is precisely this intensification: attentive consciousness of myself in the process of thinking (no matter what!), and not as previously, before the *epoché*, this accessory, inattentive consciousness of myself which accompanies any act of thought.

Now, the experience of the hyperbolic doubt and the intervention of the evil genius have the effect of transforming this natural and seemingly negligible evidence from psychological consciousness into apodictic evidence, into a metaphysical foundation. And this solely by intensifying attention. The relationship to self by coincidence which is at the root of any act of thought, which is the essence of all consciousness and which is neglected through inattention, can become, for an attentive consciousness, the radical point of departure of metaphysics on condition that the attention of consciousness manages to actualize its apodictic evidence. Consciousness of self is not the appearance of a new *object* to consciousness, nor the sudden looming up of a pure or transcendental ego, but a becoming aware of self. *Cogito* does not signify *cogito me cogitantem,* but very simply *cogito:* only this *cogito* is now as it were swollen with apodicticity.

But the true radical coincidence actualized by attention is realized still more in the *sum.* We see, in fact, the annulment of the distance which the evil genius seemed to introduce irremediably between consciousness and itself. But attention triumphs over the grand deceiver, for the evil genius cannot prevent every act of thought from being accompanied by an embryonic consciousness of self, nor especially can he prevent attention from developing this embryo into apodictic certainty: "it seems to me that I am" becomes for an attentive consciousness "I am."

Husserl was not a psychologist and was no longer interested, like his master Brentano, in this double structure of

all psychological consciousness: intentional consciousness
of objects always accompanied by implicit consciousness of
self. For Husserl, consciousness is completely intentional,
or more exactly he cannot conceive consciousness of self
otherwise than as a change of intentionality. All coincidence with self by attentive reflexion is excluded, and the
reflexive *Selbstbesinnung* perpetually ricochets as new intentionality, projects consciousness towards its world ever
more decisively. Consciousness is essentially an opening
onto the world. Caught up in its centrifugal movement it
cannot avoid losing itself in the world except by re-grasping
this world in the unity of its meaning, except by taking
refuge in a new dimension of intentionality: the transcendental, that is to say by laying out before itself the ever
more complete and more explicit spectacle of the world.

The true radical origin is aimed at through a recovery
of the world; it cannot be understood except as an ever
more total recuperation of the world: on the one side as
"total intention," as a spectacle laid out before the "disinterested spectator," on the other side as "hidden teleology" on the level of the constituting *Leistung* that gives the
world its meaning.

In the transcendental perspective of constituting intentionality, we can speak if necessary of the coincidence
of consciousness with itself, but this can mean nothing
other than the coincidence of transcendental consciousness
with the totality of its intention, that is to say with the
world. *This* coincidence is the true radical point of departure in Husserl. Obviously, it is inaccessible in fact and it
can only be aimed at. The search for the radical point of
departure can only consist in the process of the growing
radicalization of philosophy, the ever more acute crisis of
its meaning and, across it, the progressive rationalization of
reason itself, recovering its own history and its hidden tele-

ology by recovering the world. But the permanent displacement which intentionality and reduction maintain between consciousness and itself entails a permanent difference in level between the natural and the transcendental. The point of departure thus cannot be a *hold in being,* but an *act of recovery* or of transcendental constitution.

One could develop this still further, but we will limit ourselves here to a simple indication. It is striking to find in both Descartes and Husserl that no sooner is this radical beginning established than it shows itself to be *secondary* and that the apodicticity of this first act-principle is immediately colored by contingency. The Cartesian ego becomes conscious of its lack of being, of its finitude, of its dependence on the infinite Being, which in the *ordo cognoscendi* comes afterward, but which is nevertheless more primary in the *ordo essendi.* Husserl's transcendental Ego more and more acknowledges that it is secondary with respect to the contingent facticity of the *Lebenswelt,* that is to say of the non-reflexive or the pre-reflexive.

4. RADICALISM AND TRANSCENDENTALISM

Husserl, the perpetual *Anfänger,* thus discovered that he was "necessarily on the way."[20] He never stopped beginning. And, in short, this is because he never really began to end. His pathos of the *Anfang,* this feeling of never getting beyond the "beginning of the beginning,"[21] this poignant admission in his last sickness: "I have realized a weak beginning . . . I know that it is necessary for me to do everything over again from the beginning,"[22] all this shows us that the problem of the radical and primary beginning is ultimately for him rather the problem of the final truth, the *problem of the end,* in the double sense we expect: on the one hand the impossibility of putting an end to the movement of philosophy and of considering anything at all as definitely acquired, and on the other hand the problem of teleology, that is to say of an end which would not be the end aimed at unless it were already present from the beginning and already working in a latent manner from the start.

We see the enormous distance that separates Descartes from Husserl. One sought for the true beginning of what is not yet there, the other the true beginning of what is already there. The one is an inventor who wants to erase everything and to build on foundations which would be entirely his own. There is no *before* for him; the *fiat* of an attentive will is a beginning from zero, a creation *ex nihilo*. This frank and voluntary beginning implies even here a "distinction," a discontinuity of instants. Descartes the mechanist puts the universe together again piece by piece following the rational order of linear time, the time of physics, a time without a past with a consciousness without history.

Finally, Descartes and Husserl also diverge in their conception of time. The act of phenomenological uncovering implies that there is an "already there," a past, a history, and that to intend this "before" is to intend an end. Husserl, like Jaspers, is between the beginning and the end. He lives in a historicity, in situation, *in the time of consciousness,* that is to say in the time of reminiscence, for there is a latent reason to transform into a patent reason. And he also lives in the time of anticipation, because an end is intended and because this latent past already prefigures the future which is going to reveal it as past. There is here a *before* which it is *finally* necessary to unveil, or, in other words, to rediscover. The *Urstiftung* is at bottom a *Nach-*

stiftung, and to each *Urstiftung* there belongs, like a task, an *Endstiftung.*[23]

The beginning is thus for Husserl on this side of all that which we can reach as most primary and on the other side of our final aim. This is possible because at bottom everything is already there, everything is accomplished. And the intention of radicalism aims finally at reabsorbing the point of departure and every presupposition in the movement of philosophy itself. It is in this very phenomenological will to disclose what is latent that we can say Husserl Platonizes, and not, as has been asserted, in the intending and in the intuition of ideal essences. There is a problem of the beginning because we gradually become aware that everything has already begun before us and that our future, in a sense, is behind us. This is why this philosopher of the project and of intentionality turned his questioning more and more towards the past and towards history. Salvation is always anterior. Such is the profound truth where Platonic reminiscence, Christian predestination (which is, let us note, eschatology, science of the *last things*), and the hidden teleology of Husserl meet. For Descartes, on the other hand, salvation is always present; it is contained in the very act of the attentive consciousness or of the attentive will, in the instantaneous evidence.

Thus we have radicalism and radicalism: either to establish a first truth or to recover truth in a more original way. In spite of the superficial similarities which Husserl liked to point out between Descartes and himself, in spite of his care to inscribe himself in the Cartesian tradition and to develop the Cartesian ambition more faithfully than Descartes himself, we are dealing with two irreducible attitudes. We are reduced either to Cartesianize or to Platonize; and if we Platonize, either to Platonize in the transcendent sense of Plato or in the transcendental sense of

Husserl. But one thing is clear: Descartes does not lead to Husserl as to his most radical culmination, for we do not reach the transcendental by following the path of Descartes. That is why Lachelier was right in saying that Maine de Biran is "our Kant." If transcendentalism has never taken root in France in spite of the enormous influence of Kant, it is certainly due to Descartes.

Thus, the merit of Descartes was not, as Husserl thought, to have discovered transcendental subjectivity, nor was it his demerit to have immediately squandered and lost this precious acquisition, but to have attempted a radical point of departure that excluded from the start any recourse to the transcendental because the apodictic evidence that founds science is precisely the consciousness of being, the coincidence of consciousness with itself. Cartesianism and the whole French tradition of reflexive analysis which has preserved and developed it up to the present day demonstrate that transcendentalism is not the only possibility for philosophical radicalism, and at the same time this explains why until now transcendentalism has been absent from French philosophy, though we cannot say that French philosophy has been less radical because of it.

On the contrary, we can even say that transcendentalism betrays an essential lack of radicalism (among other things, by its suspicion of metaphysics as such). For the transcendentalists, human reason always escapes, in spite of everything, from a real and radical examination—we see this in Kant as well as in Husserl, but we see it also in Heidegger's ontology which claims for all that to correct Husserl on this point.

But in Descartes human reason is shaken to its foundations by the radical testing involved in the intervention of the evil genius. It is precisely this initial threat weighing on reason that triggers simultaneously both Cartesian radicalization and Cartesian metaphysics. Is not philosophical radicalism exactly proportionate to this initial menace? The radicalism of the point of departure is proportionate to the radicalism of the initial questioning of reason or of man. Husserlian transcendentalism, in spite of its very real intention of being radical, does not feel this fundamental threat directed at the very status of reason in man and in the world. Husserl's unshakeable and primary confidence in reason and science has been frequently pointed out. He substitutes for it a less serious threat—one which rules the whole phenomenological undertaking—namely, that of the loss of meaning of science. There is a "crisis of the European *sciences*" and not a crisis of *reason*.

The crisis of reason defines radicalism at the point of departure. Philosophy begins with it; the *philosophari* is always a *deinde,* an afterwards. But the radicalism of this tearing away from the *primum vivere,* the motivation of this breaking away, determines the whole ulterior movement of philosophy. In this sense the pre-reflexive truly determines the reflexive, not like a latent force or a hidden teleology, but solely through its capacity of challenging reason first of all to recover itself in the face of this threat and to situate itself in a first beginning which, by that very fact, will be radical.

REFLEXION AND CONSCIOUSNESS OF SELF

PHILOSOPHY IS DISTINGUISHED from science by a certain mode of knowledge of self, a type of knowledge that cannot be dissociated from any knowledge that wishes to throw light on its own foundations. If the Socratic precept "know thyself" constitutes the Magna Charta of philosophical "subjectivity" (its first franchise and its original emancipation), it also represents the very charter of the philosophical enterprise as a whole insofar as it is a search for a truly radical objectivity.

Reflexion is the very method of philosophy because, at least at first view, it appears that the subject cannot grasp itself except by a returning back on itself, by the recovery or the bringing to light of a radical foundation of subjectivity which up to then had remained inaccessible or unclarified.

But in this search for the subject as subject we quickly come up against fundamental alternatives whose consequences are, without any doubt, of a decisive importance for philosophy. Here any choice will lead to consequences which cannot be foreseen from the outset.

The first alternative could be formulated in this way: —Either we grasp the subject with its explicit determinations, but then it is a subject which we have transformed into an object in order to apprehend it or in order to apprehend some aspect of it; —or we disclose the subject more and more as a source that continually remains at the fringes of our consciousness, that remains implicit or unclarifiable as such. Any clarification would entail a denaturation of the subject into a new kind of object and would end in contradictory results because our reflexion meant to attain to the subject as subject. Is reflexion condemned to founder in this way between Charybdis and Scylla, between the reef of a clarified but objectified, and thus denatured, subject, and that of a merely implicit subject? Between the reef of a subject that can be attained but not as subject, and that of a subject that remains truly subject but which cannot be attained?

A second alternative bears on the double meaning of *reflexion:* —Either re-flect means to project onto a new level, and then it is the movement by which the subject, starting from a sort of original unity which cannot be grasped as such, tries to grasp itself by dissociating itself, by dividing itself or by doubling back on itself, by multiplying itself. This reflexion, by means of a centrifugal motion and by successive regressions, gradually reaches a state of greater expansion and proliferation around the original central point, a play of infinite reflections. —Or reflect means to concentrate oneself, to go from multiplicity towards unity by a centripetal motion. The subject thus moves from a state of dispersion or distraction; he turns to himself, he collects himself, simplifies himself and concentrates himself at his center. By an ascesis or by stripping himself (by "reduction," Lagneau would say), he rediscovers his immediacy, his immediation to himself, his coincidence with himself. Is reflexion condemned here also to founder between Charybdis and Scylla, between an infinite regress, which is like the cancerous growth of reflexion, and the immediation in which reflexion is purely and simply annulled and in which we remain without defense and without a criterion in face of the perhaps fallacious glamour of an unverifiable immediate?

Without claiming to decide definitively between these alternatives here, it is perhaps useful to clarify them, no longer by abstractly reconstructing pure and extreme cases, suited to bring out the problematic of reflexion, but by basing ourselves on a few philosophers who conceived their task as philosophers to be a reflexive experience. For, in a sense, modern and contemporary philosophy is engaged in a long debate on the meaning and value of reflexion, a debate which brings into conflict the meditative reflexion of a Descartes, the reflexive method of the *Treatise on the Correction of the Understanding,* Kantian transcendentalism, the *Selbstbewusstsein* of post-kantian idealism, the Kierkegaardian repetition, the reflexive analysis of Maine de Biran and of Jules Lagneau, the intuition-reflexion of Bergson, the reflexive act of Lavelle, the reflexion to the second power of Gabriel Marcel—not to forget phenomenological reflexion. In fact, in spite of appearances, in spite of the essentially intentional structure of consciousness in the phenomenological school, "the phenomenological method stays fully within acts of reflexion."[1]

Let us ask, first of all (this will be a way of clarifying our first alternative), whether the passage from implicit consciousness of self to explicit consciousness of self involves a leap or a continuity of development. Is there, to speak the language of Bergson, a difference of nature or only of degree? By observing that the essential, even unique, structure of consciousness is intentionality or "direction towards an object," phenomenology enables us to bring our question into full relief. It is clear that any conception of consciousness that gives a special place to the orientation towards the object will tend to conceive the grasping of the subject by itself as a particular mode of intentionality and to establish a radical discontinuity between the implicit and the explicit grasping of self—with the very important reservation that it is necessary to admit the existence of an implicit consciousness of self. On this point the opposition between the intentional psychology of Franz Brentano and the phenomenology of Husserl appears to us very instructive.

In his *Psychologie vom empirischen Standpunkt,* Brentano was preoccupied with determining the specificity of psychic phenomena in opposition to physical phenomena. He notes two characteristics distinctive of any psychic phenomenon:

1. *Intentionality* or "direction towards an object" (which is not necessarily a reality). "Every psychic phenomenon contains within itself something as object, though each in its own manner." In representation something is represented, in judgment something is admitted or rejected, in love something is loved. There is always the intentional presence of the object in the psychic subject.

2. Psychic phenomena are perceived only in the *interior consciousness,* that is to say in an immediately evident perception. In other words, the intentional representation of the object is always accompanied by consciousness; together with the representation of a sound one always has at the same time the representation of the representation of a sound. But, Brentano remarks, this representation of representation is conscious, like every psychic phenomenon. It thus implies a representation of representation of representation, and here arises the spectre of the infinite regress. If we wish to avoid this regress or if we do not want to stop the regress arbitrarily by admitting an *unconscious consciousness,* there is only one way out. It consists in conceiving the consciousness of hearing and the consciousness

of the object heard as constituting *one and the same phe-nomenon* (this is exactly the reasoning of Aristotle in the *De Anima*). We can only divide it into two representations by abstraction; in reality the sound is the *primary object* of the consciousness which hears (intentionality) and the consciousness of hearing is the *secondary object* (internal consciousness). The secondary object is never more than implicit or marginal (*en parego, ἐν παρέγῳ*, said Aristotle in the *Metaphysics*). It cannot be grasped as such, explicitly, except by being transformed into an intentional object, into a primary object, for the psychic can naturally, in turn, become the object of intentionality.

This is to say that we will have either implicit consciousness of self (as secondary object) or explicit consciousness of the subject transformed into a primary intentional object. It is impossible to pass from one to the other except by a leap. The explicit consciousness of self is not at all in the prolongation of immediate consciousness of self. The possibility that the latter could become the former by a continuous development is excluded. They remain incommensurable with one another in their very structure.

We know that Husserl adopted Brentano's intentionality. However, since his preoccupations were not those of a psychologist but of an epistemologist and a logician, he has no use for the sort of interior dimension of the subject that was Brentano's implicit consciousness. Consciousness of the object and consciousness of the *act* (*Erlebnis*) that intends this object, which in Aristotle and Brentano are one. phenomenon, are two in Husserl. Intentionality is now the only dimension of consciousness. "While we live so to speak in the act in question (when, for example, we lose ourselves in reading a story), then we do not notice anything of this I who is the center of reference of the accomplished acts."[2] Thus, either we intend the object or we intend the act become object in its turn; we never have the two together in the same act, because an intentional act can naturally never intend more than one object at a time. Under these conditions only reflexion can effect the grasping of consciousness by itself. There is no immediate internal consciousness—not even implicit. For Husserl, to live in the act (*erleben*) is conceived as *losing oneself in the object*. Consciousness is wholly intentional, it is wholly object. There is only one way for consciousness not to lose itself and that is to accomplish a reflexive act. Husserl says this very clearly when he analyzes the act of giving meaning: "If we accomplish the act and live so to speak in it, we naturally intend its object and not its meaning . . . This latter does not become an object except in an act of reflexive knowledge."[3]

Now phenomenological analysis (which later on will be developed under the form of the "reduction") begins precisely at the moment when one does not wish to lose himself and when one reacts against this natural and centrifugal intentionality. Phenomenology means to reverse the direction of thought, to go against the natural attitude (*widernatürlich*). This is the reflexion that makes of phenomenological analysis an essentially reflexive analysis, an "immanent analysis." "We must reflect, that is to say we must make objects of the acts themselves and of their content of immanent meaning." This content is in intentionality itself, in consciousness. The intended object as intended is "*immanent gegenwärtig*," present in the act. Thus, even by ceasing to lose ourselves in the object, thanks to reflexion on the act, we do not do away with the object; it remains always "immanent," always intentionally present.

For example: I hear a sound = I am a heard sound, I lose myself in this heard sound. Then by reflexion, I intend the act of hearing, and I then have consciousness *of hearing* a sound. But here the consciousness of oneself hearing is always accompanied by the *implicit* consciousness of the intended object, for there is no consciousness of hearing which is not consciousness of hearing something.

The situation is completely the reverse of what we find in Brentano. He showed that there was no means of hearing the sound without having the *implicit* consciousness of hearing (of oneself hearing). And Husserl tells us that there is no means of having consciousness of hearing without the sound being implicitly present. We see that Husserlian intentionality demands reflexion precisely to take the place of the immediate implicit consciousness of Brentano, and that reflexive consciousness of self is characterized by the immanent and implicit presence of the object in it.

Ought we to conclude that for Husserl in the hearing of a sound there is either *consciousness of an object* or *consciousness of an act?* Actually it would be more exact to say that we have *two different acts:* (1) either the act of hearing in the natural attitude, with the object heard, or (2) the act of reflecting on the act of hearing in the counter-natural attitude, with the object implied. It is simply a difference of intentionality: the two forms of consciousness represent a change of attitude or of "coefficient," or, as Husserl says, a loss of naiveté. "Putting in parentheses" (the reduction) is a way of rendering the implicit act explicit by reducing the too explicit object in which consciousness was entirely absorbed to an implicit state.

But the reflexive acts are comparable to the first in that we also *live* them, that they are also *Erlebnisse* like the first and that they have simply become objects in their turn.[4] "Instead of living *in* them [= these "theses," these thetic acts of the natural attitude], of effecting *them,* we perform acts of *reflexion* directed on them . . . We live henceforth exclusively in these acts of the second degree whose datum is the infinite field of absolute experiences—*the fundamental field of phenomenology.*"⁵

Reflexion enables us to attain a new "experience" in a new world of "objects" that we can describe and clarify. However, this reflexive movement continues to develop: "The reflexive operations are experiences in their turn and as such can serve as the substrata for new reflexions and so on to infinity."⁶

Hence the multiplication of reductions in the transcendental philosophy of Husserl, the network of interlocking layers and levels of reflexion. And yet at each regression there is only a new intentional consciousness of an object and not strictly speaking a consciousness of self. The existence of an immediate consciousness obviated the infinite regress in Brentano; here there is no such thing and the regress has no longer any reason to stop. To the *psychological reflexion* of the *Logische Untersuchungen* succeeds the *transcendental reflexion* of the *Cartesian Meditations,* which in turn divides into *noetic reflexion* (on the *cogito*) and *noematic reflexion* (on the *cogitatum*), etc. Reflexion is carried away by its own movement and causes a proliferation of levels of objects and corresponding *Egos*. Eugen Fink, assistant and disciple of Husserl, went so far as to glory in this proliferation as compared with Kant and to speak with pride of the "three I's" of the phenomenological reduction. And yet in this transcendental expansion we certainly never meet the subject as subject, but only another consciousness *of the world,* because consciousness is always consciousness *of* . . . Consciousness, by the fact of its uniquely intentional structure, preserves its centrifugal dynamism even in the most searching reflexion. Thus it maintains in itself an insurmountable "knot of opacity," as Sartre says in the penetrating criticism he made of Husserl's transcendental Ego.[7] The Sartrian radicalization was necessary for consciousness conceived on the one hand as a "nothingness" and on the other hand as a "consciousness (of) self" to become fully translucid. The knot of opacity can be eliminated only by the reintroduction of an immediate consciousness of self.

Husserl remained fundamentally objectivistic and the phenomenological method makes it forever impossible to enclose consciousness within itself. The problem of reflexion and of consciousness of self always remained for him the problem of a consciousness opened onto the world, intending transcendent essences, fundamentally centrifugal. Consciousness has no interiority, and the phenomenological reduction tends to reveal better and better to a consciousness less and less lost in the world, more and more a "disinterested spectator," a progressively more complete and explicit view of the objective world that it intends.

The layers of this objective world are unfolded by the subject, but because of its submission to the object this subject is sent back to the end of a never-achieved regression and of an infinite repetition, towards a source as primary and radical as it is effectively inaccessible. If the phenomenological philosophy of Husserl remains open and unfinished, this is because it reflects the very characteristics of this consciousness which it defines as open to the world. Phenomenology appears as the philosophy of infinite reflexion because it is wholly the intending of a consciousness of self at once necessary and impossible.

By beginning with the first alternative concerning the explicit or implicit consciousness of self, we have arrived at the very heart of the second alternative concerning the immediate or the infinite regress. The two are in fact intimately related. It is now indispensable to specify the notions of immediacy and undivided reflexion.

The philosopher has a deep, ever present, and well justified suspicion with regard to the immediate. Without the verification of an objectifying consciousness or reflexion, it seems that no knowledge can enjoy the seal of true philosophical objectivity. An immediate consciousness would thus require that a similar look be directed on itself in order to receive freedom of the city in philosophy, and reflexive consciousness would have to be conceived as a sort of *autopsia,* an inspection or verification of self. In this perspective all immediacy or coincidence of consciousness with itself can only appear as a falling back from the reflexive to the pre-reflexive level, from consciousness of self to a state of irremediably subjective unconsciousness. The mistrust of philosophers for any form of psychologism is rooted in this notion of immediacy. But are we really bound to this "optical" conception of self-consciousness as a look directed at itself, and to the notion of immediacy that it implies? If reflexion were not a look, and if it were rather interpreted in terms of action, would it not be possible to conceive a passage from the immediate to the reflexive in which the reflexive would still be a form of the immediate and in which the immediate would not be necessarily and solely psychological?

On the other hand, we like to think that psychological consciousness (immediate or non-reflexive consciousness) is the only form of self-consciousness without redoubling, in which consciousness coincides very naturally with itself. And since philosophy is essentially reflexion, it clearly implies a redoubling of consciousness. However (in spite of the apparent contradiction in terms), has philosophy no undivided immediacy even for reflexive or explicit consciousness? Such an undivided self-consciousness would obviously have psychological roots, but it is possible to show that it at once goes beyond simple psychological immediacy, and that a reflexion which would not be a look but an action could operate a kind of progression of the immediate to a higher level that would be truly philosophical.

It is precisely in this sense that we have to understand reflexion in the French tradition of what it has become customary to call *reflexive analysis,* whether it is a question of the intellectual act of attention in Descartes, of the experience of muscular effort in Maine de Biran, or of Bergsonian intuition, which is more willing than seeing, more creation than contemplation. The paradox of this reflexive *analysis* which, precisely in so far as it is act and effort, is essentially *synthetic,* has been justly pointed out. The reflexion which leads to the Cartesian *cogito,* or to the Biranian *volo,* is not a simple introspective analysis. And yet, by immediately transcending the psychological from which it begins, it is not at all oriented in a transcendental direction (neither in the Kantian nor in the Husserlian sense).[8] It is not a question of discovering by analysis something hidden or elemental, some implicit structure (something non-reflexive, contemporary phenomenology would say). It is rather a question of bringing out, *synthetically and immediately,* explicit consciousness of self *in* the very act of reflexion.

For example, Descartes grounds consciousness of self in the *cogito* which is reflexion in a very special sense. When the methodic doubt pushes back the external world and transforms it, so to speak, into an implicit object, Descartes refuses in effect to see the world and to *see himself* as an object. He is looking for a primary certitude which is an immediate evidence. His approach is essentially centripetal; it does not aim at revealing latent riches to an unchanging spectator, but at developing or making explicit the act of the mind itself by rendering it conscious of itself in its very exercise, and by thus promoting in it a superior immediacy. It is by an effort of attention (and not of reduction) that Descartes becomes aware, at the very instant when he doubts, of the actuality of his thought, i.e., of the act of his becoming conscious. And as distinguished from psychological immediacy, the immediacy of the *cogito* possesses immediately in a truly privileged manner all the characteristics of apodicticity required for valid philosophical knowledge. On the other hand, this reflexion does not reveal the least trace of division into reflecting consciousness (or subject) and reflected (or objectified) consciousness. The *Cogito* does not mean *cogito me cogitantem*. It only means the synthetic positing or specifying (by attention or intensification) of an immediate and implicit consciousness. The act of thinking does not grasp a thinking consciousness as a new object which up to then had been thinking unconsciously or "naively." Rather it grasps an act, it grasps a consciousness which is wholly and completely this act, it grasps itself. But by rendering the *cogitata* (or the world) implicit by the *epoché* of the doubt, he permitted implicit consciousness to be (as act) the only "object" of consciousness, in short to specify itself as an act of self-consciousness, as a reflexive grasping of self (of the subject as subject).

This consciousness of consciousness avoids the reflexive division only by actualizing itself as *a becoming conscious,* without any detachment from the initial immediacy, by transcending its psychological character (its instantaneousness) without sacrificing its immediate character. "By the word thought," said Descartes, "I understand all that which occurs in us in such a way that we perceive it immediately by ourselves." The act of thinking is assured, consolidated, and experienced in its own accomplishment. Reflexion brings out the immediate in an act and in an actualization, and thus in the actual present. That is why it would be impossible to say: *Cogitabam ergo eram* or *cogitabo ergo ero*. In fact, if it is deprived of the reference to *present* and immediate consciousness, in other words to the act of becoming conscious, consciousness of self either is redoubled once more or it—rather—vanishes. The total disappearance of the apodictic certainty of the *cogito* as soon as it is detached from the present testifies to this eloquently. The leap between the implicit and the explicit which we found in Brentano is no longer found here between implicit consciousness of self and explicit consciousness of self, but between the present on the one hand and the past or future on the other—between immediacy and division, which is perfectly natural.

Moreover, in the act of becoming conscious of the *cogito ergo sum,* reflexive consciousness preserves its undivided immediacy and advances it only because it is *consciousness of being* (consciousness that I am). Is there a better proof that we are not dealing with a transcendental consciousness? The transcendental, in Husserl as in Kant, is obtained by putting in parentheses any empirical position on existence, any factual reality, by de-actualization. On the contrary, by making itself explicit in the *cogito,* implicit consciousness becomes consciousness of being, consciousness of my existence. It is situated as an experience in being and in factual reality. I become conscious that my act of thinking "needs only itself to "exist" and to be assured of its existence. That is the very definition of substance according to Descartes. The "substantialism" for which Descartes is so often reproached was thus originally (before it developed into the substantialist realism of the *res cogitans*) nothing but the expression of the immediacy of a reflexive consciousness. The act of thinking is a *substance* because it can be grasped without redoubling and without an infinite regress. And it can be grasped because it is, immediately, consciousness of being. It is substance in the sense of *causa sui*, in the precise sense in which the anti-substantialist Maine de Biran defines the ego as cause and action, and not as thing.

Thus, in synthetic reflexive analysis the immediate is actualized in the reflected or (what comes to the same thing) reflexion is a way of attaining an explicit and founded immediate. To make it explicit is to realize the amplification or intensification of an embryonic consciousness, of a consciousness so to speak implicit because infinitesimal. It is not surprising that Leibniz, the philosopher of continuity, had a similar conception of reflexion, that he refused to admit a gap between the implicit and the explicit, between perception and apperception, and that in the *New Essays* he based the identity of the ego on the intimate and immediate feeling it has of its own actions.

Maine de Biran in his turn realized an identical actualization in the immediate apperception of the primitive fact. From the implicit "animal" to the explicit "human," the ego is realized synthetically in the act of effort and attention. All division is avoided since the ego is really *causa sui* and truly has no need of anything besides itself to exist. "The soul," said Maine de Biran, "does not perceive other things because it is but only because it first perceives itself, that is to say because it exists for itself or because it is *ego*." As in Brentano, it is the existence of immediate consciousness that suppresses the redoubling regression *ad infinitum*. But on the contrary, this consciousness of self is an apperception and not a marginal or muted accompaniment of all consciousness of objects. It is truly an explicit consciousness of self. And what is more, in opposition to Husserl who attained explicit consciousness by muting or suspending the object, a Maine de Biran integrates the consciousness of objects the more indissolubly into the consciousness of the ego, because the primitive fact is the *relation* between a hyperorganic force and an organic resistance, between a subject and an object, both fully explicit.

If the passage from the implicit immediate to the reflexive immediate is thus realized without a leap and without an infinite regress, this amounts to saying that the immediate realizes itself or makes itself explicit. The immediate is thus no longer simply the primary and marginal datum, as in Brentano; it is, like the "immediate given" of Bergson, that which is created or re-created by a long effort of intuition, attention, or reflexion. The immediate is a synthetic "datum" because it *is given* to itself. Bergson's profound ego, the ego which is free and which lasts, is not the original still implicit and unconscious (instinctive) vital élan; it is the creative élan, reactivated thanks to a "creation of self by self" (*causa sui*).

Once more we see the solidarity of our initial alternatives affirmed. The examination of the problem of immediacy led us to the question of the implicit and explicit self. But our short inquiry does not terminate merely in this set-to. It seems that reflexive analysis carries with it a solution of these alternatives, at least as we have formulated them. A continuity of progression is possible from the implicit to the explicit, and the explicit self is not necessarily a self denatured by objectification. The redoubling of consciousness and the infinite regress are not inherent to all authentic reflexion, because it is possible to reflect while safeguarding the immediate. And the immediate is not merely psychological, because it is possible to assume and to found a reflexive immediation.

We have tried to clarify somewhat the problematic of self-consciousness, particularly the passage from implicit to explicit consciousness. In doing so we have sketched very roughly the opposition between two types of reflexion, one

of which would characterize the method of phenomenological analysis and the other the method of reflexive analysis:
(1) a reflexion based on intention (intentionality), and (2)
a reflexion based on attention or effort. Or in other words:
(1) a recuperating reflexion (explicitating recovery of the
implicit), and (2) an amplifying or dilating reflexion (intensification of consciousness).

In both cases reflexion aims at putting consciousness in
possession of itself. But if, in reflexion, the orientation towards the object is privileged, and if intentionality is the
only structure of consciousness, consciousness is projected
outside itself and dispossessed of itself by its very essence.
A recuperation is necessary. Intentionality very naturally
requires phenomenological reduction precisely in order to
fill this role. Consciousness, imprisoned in its own intentionality, cannot escape completely losing itself in the intended object except by taking refuge—its only way out—
in a new dimension of intentionality: namely, the transcendental. But, since the turning back on itself perpetually ricochets in new intentionality, according to the
phenomenologists, either consciousness no longer has any
tie to being or it is ontologically defined as nothingness (in
Sartre). There is no longer any place for a transcendentalism or a "meontology" (according to the expression of
Jean Wahl), though the philosophy of nothingness is nothing but an extreme form of transcendentalism.[9]

In amplifying reflexion, attention renders an adequation of consciousness with itself immediately possible. By
being intensified without loss of continuity, it little by
little enters into possession of its own powers. This centripetal dynamism concentrates consciousness in itself without it being necessary to empty it of being and of its own
being in order to put it in the presence and possession of
itself. Automatically the transcendental question is super-

seded, at least as concerns the problem of self-consciousness. Since this question presupposes the primacy of the object and an objective epistemology, it can only be posed and justified on the level of the consciousness of objects. It only becomes necessary and central for the problem of self-consciousness for those who believe that self-consciousness can only be approached mediately, through the consciousness of objects or as a new kind of consciousness of objects.

Certainly there is no reason to contest the fact that intentionality is the *primary*, original, and natural structure of consciousness, because man is first of all, naturally, next to things, in the world, incarnated, engaged. It is the merit of phenomenology to have shown this, to have eliminated the image of a container-consciousness, and to have expelled represented or intended objects outside of consciousness. Consequently, it is very true that the turning towards self, reflexion, *explicit* consciousness of self is *secondary* (but at the same time more original and more "radical"). To the extent that self-consciousness is a *recovery*, it may well at first sight appear artificial and against nature—but only the better to rediscover the *natura naturans* beyond the *natura naturata*. Any return to self is *widernatürlich* (Husserl) and "goes against the natural inclination" (Bergson). It requires the ascesis of the doubt or of the "reduction" (in Husserl's sense as well as in the sense of Lagneau) and the sustained hyperorganic, and hyperpsychological effort of the will. In this sense self-consciousness is always para-physical, anti-physical or meta-physical.

But to go from this to the affirmation that this turning-back is only a derivative or a mode of the intentional project, to say that attention has only a psychological value or that it derives from intention, in short to say that there is no reflexive immediacy, is a decisive step which Husserl seems to take gladly but in which we cannot follow him. In fact this amounts, in one way or another, to taking our primary attitude vis-à-vis the world too seriously and to putting metaphysics back under the tutelage of a kind of "physics."

Phenomenology thus gives preference to the primary and natural attitude. Even when it does not reach an explicit ontology we can say that it tends to identify what is primary in the *ordo cognoscendi* with what is primary in the *ordo essendi*. It qualifies as "naive" the attitude by which, carried away by intentionality, we immerse ourselves in objects. According to phenomenology, "naiveté" consists in losing oneself in objects, but intentionality as such remains safe. In fact, is there not in intentionality itself a more profound and more concealed naiveté, at least insofar as it is a question of consciousness of self?[10] Perhaps it is not enough to pass from the object to the transcendental subject in order to attain a non-naive and more original consciousness of self.

Is not the only way to "sophisticate" consciousness radically to show it that it can reach itself without passing through objects, and thus to reveal its own consistency and its own ontological weight? Reflexive analysis asks attention to furnish this access or this reflexive turning back to being, and it discovers, as we have pointed out, the primary ontological assurance in consciousness of being. If this immediate consciousness of self were only implicit, it would of course never be the primary tie between consciousness and its own being or between consciousness and being in general. In this sense we could say: Intentionality is the *chronologically* primary structure of consciousness, but reflexion is its *ontologically* primary or original structure.

However, this ontological hold cannot satisfy us today under the form in which it was conceived by a Descartes, a Bergson, or, closer to us, a Lavelle. Perhaps consciousness of self introduces us less to a certitude in Being than to consciousness of our *human condition,* and even more of an essentially threatened condition. Is it not necessary to re-think the problem of self-consciousness within the frame-work of an analysis of the human *situation* rather than within the framework of a classical, essentialist ontology? It is certain that consciousness of being can lead as well to the Being of classical ontology as to the "being-in-the-world" or to the "situation" of contemporary philosophies. The whole problem must be taken up again.

Reflexive analysis has a true conception of reflexion, but perhaps it has an outmoded or insufficiently elabo-rated notion of being, whereas phenomenology may have a true notion of being but a too objectivist or insufficient conception of reflexion. It is by mutually fecundating one another that these two methods will be able to trace a new path in philosophical thought. The first would establish the immediate and explicit relationship to self; the second, the relationship to objects. Not that they would be simply complementary and divide the total area of consciousness into two juxtaposed sectors; this would be to reintroduce within the bosom of consciousness an impassable gap simi-lar to what we rejected earlier. On the contrary, we would say that phenomenological intentionality ought to locate itself within the reflexive structure of consciousness which, because it is more radical, has a kind of ontological primacy with respect to intentionality. Far from interpreting re-flexion by means of intentionality as Husserl, Sartre, and Merleau-Ponty do, we must do the opposite: interpret in-tentionality on the basis of reflexion. Intentionality can very well be revelatory and constitutive of the objective world; it none the less remains that the immediately re-flexive consciousness of self is a *constituting power* more original, a fact more primitive, than intentionality.

Here is, therefore, the place to repeat with Maine de Biran: "There are men who suppose that the personality or knowledge of oneself is not a necessary condition of intelligence . . . The same vice lies in the philosophy of Condillac and German metaphysics, namely: the supposition that it is *not essential to the intelligence to know itself* in order to exist as intelligence."

GOING BEYOND
METAPHYSICS

METAPHYSICS IS CONTESTED. It always has been. It was contested by the sophists, by the "philodoxists" or the "misologists" of whom Plato spoke, by the skeptics and the relativists, by the empiricists and positivists—by men of science, by theologians, by artists, and by honest men.

It is contested today more than ever. It seems clear that the era of the great metaphysical systems has gone. The distrust or the disdain for systematic constructions, for metaphysical intemperance, for the *Träume eines Geistersehers*, is universal. Nobody has the courage any more or the taste to undertake again the enterprises of a Plato, a Spinoza, or a Hegel. Metaphysics as the science of the beyond is not even the beautiful, nostalgic dream of a few epigoni any more. Since Kant, modern philosophy has directed its efforts patiently and obstinately to recuperating —and adoring—what during the centuries metaphysics had burned, namely the *hic et nunc,* history, time and movement, contingency, experience, the sensible, in a word the this-side, the *Diesseitigkeit.* A painful and uneasy attempt to go against the current of a centuries-old atavism.

Metaphysics is contested. It is natural that it should be so; this is in order. Not simply that it is normal that it be misunderstood or that it be abused in proportion to its attempt to incarnate a higher value; but it is as if the contesting of metaphysics (or of philosophy in general) were inscribed in its very nature. This is already true of any given metaphysics; every philosopher must know that his system will be discussed and inevitably contested. In the course of history all the systems have been. But this is even more true of metaphysics as such, as a philosophical discipline. Its legitimacy never ceases to be questioned anew.

Metaphysics is contested. This is a fact, but is the fact justified? The question is to know whether it is contested from within or from without, by playing the metaphysical game or by remaining outside it. There is the type of questioning that falls short of what it questions. And there is the type that means to go beyond by basing itself on the very thing it questions—this is the only fruitful and legitimate way of contesting: by going beyond. It is in this sense that Aristotle contests Plato: he traverses him in order to go beyond him in a new direction, towards a truth that is more true, *amicus Plato*. In this sense likewise Spinoza contests Descartes, or Kant contests Leibniz, or Hegel, Schelling. But to contest *a* metaphysics or *the* metaphysics by denouncing it as a simple illusion, by declaring it null and void, is to condemn oneself to remaining deliberately on this side of the impulse that gave it birth. In short, the anti-metaphysician contests by refusing; the metaphysician contests by going beyond.

But if philosophy progresses from contestation to contestation, from correction to correction, it can happen occasionally that the most profound revolutions signify the surpassing of a whole portion of the philosophical past. In spite of their oppositions, Platonism, Aristotelianism and Stoicism are put in question as a block by the Cartesian *cogito;* in the same way Kant wants to go beyond the whole of what has since been called pre-critical philosophy, and from Kant to the present we have seen more than once the attempt to go beyond metaphysics as such, all metaphysics of all times.

At the same time we note that metaphysics itself is born of questioning the everyday and original experience of the world, the experience which it invites us precisely to transcend in the direction of a beyond. Apart from the chance arrangement of his works, Aristotle gave to the term "metaphysics" a false etymology (beyond nature and physics) which in fact corresponded rather exactly to the aim of metaphysics at that time.

Thus, if we can say that metaphysics is already by itself questioning and going-beyond, the notion of a going-beyond of metaphysics will not appear too strange. Does not the élan of transcendence impressed on philosophical research by Plato, and prolonged across the centuries, underlie both the movement that gives rise to metaphysics and the movement that contests it by going beyond it? Would it not be possible to recapture the unity of this movement, to experience the signification and the scope of this going-beyond, and to mark its culmination in contemporary philosophy? Would this not be on the one hand to comprehend the purpose of metaphysics, in the very act that contests and goes beyond it, and on the other hand to fix the conditions of possibility and legitimacy of the metaphysical enterprise today? Is not the integration of the history of philosophy into philosophy the only means of remaining faithful to it while detaching oneself from its hold? The only one who can validly speak of going beyond metaphysics is the one who adopts its approach precisely in order to try to carry it more truly along towards its goal, who attempts to discern or to invent this goal by espousing ever more closely the winding and sometimes hesitant path it follows across history. There is no short-cut without losing the sense of direction, and especially the élan. We can speak of going beyond metaphysics only if we interpret the history of philosophy as being itself the effort of going beyond metaphysics.

Since metaphysics is going-beyond, will not going beyond metaphysics lead us to a sort of philosophy of going-beyond that would give us definitively the actual possibility of metaphysics and its most precise definition? Will we not see the questioning of metaphysics lead into a philosophy of questioning?

It is therefore necessary to be critical with respect to the metaphysics of the past. But as opposed to the positivists who consider the criticism of metaphysics to be its negation and abandonment, we will say with Kant that the criticism of metaphysics contains "the metaphysics of metaphysics,"[1] that is to say a metaphysics more conscious of itself, of its situation, of its aims and of its limits: "Metaphysik ist nicht Wissenschaft, nicht Gelehrsamkeit, sondern bloss der sich selbst kennende Verstand."[2]

1. METAPHYSICS AS GOING-BEYOND TOWARDS THE BEYOND

Under its first impetus, philosophical thought is simply metaphysics because it is going-beyond. It has been said that it begins in wonder. In fact, reflexion arises when the world of completely natural evidences is found to be contestable, when it explodes so to speak, when what was taken for reality itself is transformed into appearance in the name of a reality of another order that one feels required to study or expose. Philosophical thought is never simple explicitation, simple analysis, pure observation or constatation. An initial amazement marks the opening of a new dimension, of a transcendence. By a movement of de-focusing, the world becomes disarticulated and is shown in relief, because, within a reality that was seen up to that time as flat, there appear dimly seen shapes which shift the center of perspective on reality away from the original perspective towards a point which for the moment is anticipated rather than grasped. The world is reorganized from another point of view whose discovery and formulation is precisely the job of philosophy.

This movement of transcendence constitutes metaphysics. From the time of its birth in the West, metaphysics has been inseparable from this dynamism of thought breaking with "reality" in order to go on towards another, more essential, and more fundamental reality. This going-beyond is first of all manifested as a detaching of thought, as an upward-moving élan, ascending, transcending. True being would be something towards which one raises oneself up, something that elevates man and liberates the wings of the soul. The metaphysician would be a man who emerges from the cave, who lifts up his head towards the light, who looks at the sky: the soul frees itself from an excessive natural weight, and thought, from the grip of first evidences. We understand how the philosopher could take himself for an exile from heaven, one banished from the beyond, only too happy to be able, thanks to metaphysics or "superior physics," to escape again from his earthly prison "towards his dear fatherland."

This dynamism of thought developed at the beginnings of Greek philosophy with reference to the physical problem, the natural explanation of the *physis* (φύσις). There is nothing astonishing in the fact that this going-beyond gave birth to metaphysics. Behind the incessant changes of the *physis* "is revealed a sub-understood,"[3] is traced little by little the substructure of a more stable world of a *kosmos* (κόσμος), of an eternal, intelligible, and by that very fact divine, order. Underpinning the "physical" world, a metaphysical cosmos is given as a truer, more essential world, the world of intelligible forms and essences. Then begins the fight against sensible evidence in the name of superior evidences. On the basis of the world of being, at first only glimpsed but then seen clearer and clearer, sense knowledge appears now only as a *doxa* (δόξα) and wavers in inconsistency. Or, more exactly, natural and sensible evidence takes its secondary place in a universe that transcends it. To transcend *doxa* is to understand how it arises, to retrace the origin of the sensible world and its inadequate knowledge.

Metaphysical transcending put the Greeks in possession of a world in which being is intelligible, in which being is defined by its fundamental agreement with thought, a thought become more demanding. The metaphysical world realized the coherence and unity of intelligence, language, being, and even the divine. The solution of the problem of the *physis* was thus a metaphysics, what we call today a metaphysics of the object, a metaphysics of essences or an ontology. This transcendent world is apprehended by a knowledge that is itself transcendent, that is to say that has raised itself to the (divine) level of the reality to be known. In this sense philosophy is an effort of divinization, of immortalization or of reintegration to a divine world within which the intellect and being truly find themselves on an equal footing. In these conditions neither the intellect nor language are problems. So long as they are purified by the ascesis of metaphysical going-beyond, the *logos* (λόγος) or the *nous* (νοῦς) are from the beginning instruments for revealing being, because being is reason. The intellect is rooted in being—it is immobile like it—and man can base himself on his intellect because it gives answers without itself ever being problematic.

One can even say that such is the secret ideal of metaphysics: this perfect adequation of being (grasped in its essence as beyond appearances) and thought of the *on* (ὄν) and of the *logos*. Each time one can say that the whole of the real is rational and that the whole of the rational is real, it will appear that one has attained the perfection of ontology, in short the *terminus of the going-beyond,* the true absolute. On the plane of the metaphysics of being, in fact, it will be impossible to have, after this first transcendence, still another going-beyond of being. The evidences of intelligibility are themselves ontological, therefore ultimate, and a meta-metaphysics has rigorously no sense. The metaphysics of being cannot be transcended, as if by definition.

2. GOING BEYOND METAPHYSICS

However, metaphysics is contested and remains problematic. Is not the perfect adequation of being and the intellect somewhat disquieting? Even if we forget that being is immobile and unmoveable! Does not this eternal *kosmos* contaminate the intellect itself? Does it not imprison it in its own immobility? Is the intellect repose? And can *philo*-sophy, which insofar as it is *erōs* (ἔρως) is restless, immobilize itself in the dogmatism of the *sophia?* By guaranteeing the intellect a hold on being, has not metaphysics given being a hold on the intellect? It is as if the intellect "took hold"—in the way ice or cement takes hold.

But is intelligence truly tied thus to cosmic and physical reality? Is it a question of philosophical knowledge tearing itself away from the sensible world in order to bind itself to an intelligible world? There is a transcending from the physical to the metaphysical, but the intellect has simply changed masters: *it has not gone beyond itself.* Is it not this in which the dynamism of questioning and detachment is expressed in knowledge? Intelligible evidence appears ultimate only because the intellect ordered itself to intelligible being without reflecting on it, without questioning itself as to what intelligence is. The Greeks discovered intelligence as a nature, as a cosmic reality. Does it not have to go beyond itself as nature in order to grasp itself truly as intelligence?

The transcendent dynamism of metaphysics thus cannot stop yet. It will suffice that the ties between intelligence and the cosmos be distended for this dynamism to rebound to the level of intelligence itself. If intelligence becomes problematic, it detaches itself in respect to itself and the intelligible evidences, contested, will need a new foundation; the cosmos will no longer be their natural support. After the metaphysics of being (metaphysics in the proper sense of the term) new perspectives are opened up. A going-beyond of metaphysics is henceforth possible; better, it is required by the intellect's need to understand itself. In place of letting itself be situated by being or of being ordered to the cosmos, the intellect, letting go of itself and putting its own evidence in question to itself, becomes aware that it is not so evident as it thought and attempts to recognize its situation as intellect.

Here we find metaphysics questioning itself. Its ultimate value is suspended and must be founded. It is the intellect which takes this task on itself and determines to solve it; it refuses to be immobilized and recovers its élan. It becomes conscious of not being first or "unborn" as Plotinus would say. By a redoubled going-beyond it can elevate itself above itself to a supertranscendence that would explain its genesis, as the metaphysical world explained the genesis of the physical world and the sensible "evidences." Thus the path of meta-metaphysics is opened up.

However, this movement can also go in the opposite direction. Since it begins by questioning the intimate and natural connection between intelligence and the cosmos, it implies the questioning of the meta-*physical* character of philosophy. The terms "transcendence" or "going-beyond," spatial and physical metaphors, can no longer be used except with caution. The metaphysics of being assigned to the intellect the "place" of its efficaciousness, its "natural" place: the *topos hyperouranios* (τόπος ὑπερουράνιος), in the words of the *Phaedrus*. The transcending of meta-*physics* will tend to tear the intellect away from any place, to detach it from its cosmic ties, to break with the metaphysics of the object in order to pose its problem as one of *foundation:* not to situate it within the cosmos, but in relationship to it. It will no longer be a question of the philosopher looking elsewhere, of fleeing towards the beyond, towards that which is outside and above, but of returning towards the interior and towards what is this-side. The movement of transcending is still a conversion, but, this time, in the sense of a return, of a regression towards what is original, towards the foundation: metaphysics in reverse, or a kind of *transdescendence.*[4]

With the help of a few historical examples let us outline the movement of transcending in these two orientations.

3. META-METAPHYSICS AND SUPER-TRANSCENDENCE

Already Plato, in the movement of his ascending dialectic, did not stop at the world of Ideas. He carried us on *epekeina tês ousias* (ἐπέκεινα τῆς οὐσίας), beyond the metaphysical world of the Intelligibles up to the Good, the source of being, existence, and truth. And Glaucon cries: "What divine *hyperbole!*"[5]

Neo-platonism in its turn, faithful to this specifically Platonic aspiration, made a final attempt, at the end of antiquity, to go beyond Hellenic metaphysics. Plotinus remains a Greek in preserving the identification of being and intelligence, but, in contrast to Aristotle, he no longer admits that the intellect is the first and immobile principle or that it is plunged in contemplation of itself (thought of thought). It is movement and consequently there is a genesis of intelligence, because to say that it moves itself is to say that it is oriented towards its beginning and that it is a view of the One. The dynamism of this tendency towards the One constitutes intelligence as intelligence. This bursting upward of the intelligence marks a decisive transcendence of Greek metaphysics. For the first time the intellect is no longer ordered to the physical cosmos, nor to the intelligible object, but to the supertranscendent source that lies beyond it. In fact, the One is neither cosmic nor the object of the intellect; it is simply the principle of its intelligent activity. Nor is it a being; "it is always more than everything we can think of it."[6]

Plato transcended physics by a metaphysics. Plotinus is the first to transcend intelligence in us by showing its foundation in the form of the principle of its genesis. He raises himself thus to a *metaphysics of the intellect* which is a sort of metaphysics of metaphysics itself. In this respect, since it is not a transcending of physics, it ought to be called, rather, *meta-noetics*.

The intellect becomes aware of what it is by recognizing its situation in the world. This situation in which it is no longer first, constitutes it precisely as intelligence. The intellectual evidences or the truth of being are no longer the ultimate or self-evident evidences. They come from above and the intellect turns towards them, orients itself with respect to this transcendence in order to grasp the intelligible and to unite itself intimately with it.

By placing the first principle beyond the intellect and beyond being, the neo-platonic meta-metaphysics enters the realm of the ineffable, that which is beyond language, the nothingness which is more than being and the silence which is more than speech. Philosophy, cut off from Greek cosmological intellectualism, then has the task of leading us beyond the intellect, not again (and in this Plotinus remains Greek) to devaluate the intellect or to deny intelligibility, but to found it and to grasp it at its source. However, the superabundant fullness of this superessential nothingness sensitizes us (so to speak) to the upper limits of intelligibility. We can say with Paul Decoster that Plotinus "was the first to trace the organic schema of all future metaphysics."[7]

This almost frenzied transcending towards a super-transcendence is accentuated in Pseudo-Denys the Aeropagite and in the tradition of apophatic or negative theology. Here we assist at the breakdown of language. Greek metaphysics, and especially Aristotelianism, was based on the perfect adequation of language and being. Language was natural: sensible language revealed sensible reality to us; intelligible language revealed intelligible reality. This is why language posed no problem. Pseudo-Denys experienced the inadequacy of language to express divine super-transcendence, and perceived that in relation to it rational language broke down and became an indirect and metaphorical language. Even the qualification "intelligible" is henceforth inadequate to its "object" and remains below the level of the absolutely ineffable transcendence. The sensible and coarse images, for example, that Holy Scripture uses to designate the divinity, serve better in his view to mark the distance which separates us from the inaccessible, than the intelligible designation which, because it is intelligible, is likely to be thought adequate even though it is only an image, and an inadequate image at that. At the same time negation, which is rupture, is "closer" to super-transcendence than the affirmation which believes itself to be union. But this "proximity" means here that the real, impassible distance that is the situation of the intellect, is better respected. To understand that God is incomprehensible is the maximal approach to understanding, but this comes to situating language, and thus for the first time creating a *metaphysics of language* (of the *logos,* and conjointly, since it is a question of Christian philosophy, of the *Logos*). Meta-noetics shows that it implies a *meta-logic.*

This result clarifies our investigation considerably. We see that going beyond metaphysics consists in the very consciousness of the situation of the intellect and of language, and that this consciousness arises at the precise moment when the dissociation of being and thought, of the super-essential God and the intellect, takes place.

Thus neo-platonic metaphysics does not guide the intellect and language to transcendental heights; it situates them in relation to transcendence. The intellect is no longer natural or cosmic; it is no longer naturally tied to its object. Language is no longer natural and directly revelatory of its object. The metaphysical problem of the intellect and of language, that is to say their foundation, is henceforth open. It was necessary to get beyond cosmological naturalism and Greek metaphysics, to break them open, in order to pose this problem of the foundation and to move ahead towards its solution.

It is striking and significant to observe in the Platonist Pseudo-Denys that the transcendence of metaphysics leads to a revalorization and rehabilitation of the sensible. On the level of language, the sense-image is in effect superior to the intelligible "image." Transcending the beyond brings us back to the this-side and teaches us to see it differently, to situate it differently. The sensible is not only something to be gone beyond; it can also be the place where metaphysics takes place, or at least where it is expressed and formulated, because it is also the place where the *Logos* is incarnated. Such is the point, for man, to which going beyond metaphysics leads.

The superessential God is beyond metaphysics, but is inaccessible in his supertranscendence. To understand that he is inaccessible[8] is for man to understand that his own language remains below the level of God and that it can communicate only indirectly with its object. The object is more beyond; knowledge is more on this side. Metametaphysics itself leads to metaphysics in reverse.[9] The metaphysics of the intellect and of language inaugurates the *metaphysics of knowledge* that it will later on, as theory or critique of knowledge, oppose to classical metaphysics, forgetting that the critique of knowledge is valid only as a new metaphysics, as a going-beyond of metaphysics.

4. METAPHYSICS OF CONVERSION AND TRANSCENDENCE TOWARDS THE INTERIOR

Even earlier Augustine had drawn his own conclusions from the ruptures in neo-platonic and Christian thought and was led to go beyond the metaphysics of the object and of exteriority in a different direction. His lived experience of conversion showed him the impossibility of a continuous metaphysical ascent towards God (in the manner of Plotinus): to attain God it is necessary to humiliate oneself and, by returning to oneself, to humble the rebellious will. This is, in the words of Gilson,[10] a "metaphysics of conversion" in which the going-beyond is operated by a liberation from the external world, from all that diverts or disperses the soul by separating it from God. "In teipsum redi, in interiore homine habitat veritas."[11] A new direction is assigned to the metaphysical élan, for the first time with such clarity: by a conversion *ab exterioribus ad interiora*. The soul is the mysterious place of a presence that overflows it, that upholds it and situates it: *Deus interior intimo meo*. Augustine, the Platonist, also rehabilitated lived experience in metaphysics and laid out before the soul the inexhaustible possibilities of interior transcendence.

This movement of transcending by going within, which is properly Augustinian, is prolonged across history and remains visible and living in all the metaphysics of interiority: in Maine de Biran and in the French tradition of reflexive analysis, in Lagneau and Bergson, in Paul Decoster, the metaphysician of "conversion to the intrinsic,"[12] in Lavelle, for whom metaphysics is the "science of spiritual intimacy."[13] And Bergson will say of Maine de Biran and of the metaphysics of interiority (something similar to what

Decoster said of Plotinus): "We can ask if the path this philosopher has opened up is not the one definitive way of metaphysics."[14]

However, even while it is oriented towards the interior, this transcendence of Augustine remains no less a movement towards what is above: *ab inferioribus ad superiora,* towards a *Deus superior summo meo.* The ascending élan given by Plato has not, across neo-platonism and beyond the rupture of conversion, lost its force. It is maintained in Augustine and in the whole tradition that comes from him.[15]

5. METAPHYSICS IN REVERSE

With modern philosophy, metaphysics is decidedly headed for a new destiny. Up to now going-beyond, as we have seen, was meant to lead man towards true reality. Descartes and Kant inaugurated a metaphysics of the radical foundation: in the celebrated image of the *Principles,* metaphysics represents the *roots* of the tree. It is still a question of going beyond the metaphysics of being and of essences, but even more of founding human reason and truth. The experience of methodical doubt marks the decisive rupture with the metaphysics of the object, but it is not of itself capable of leading to the going-beyond of traditional metaphysics in the direction of the problem of the radical foundation. It is the properly "metaphysical" or "hyperbolic" doubt that inaugurates this and makes it possible. The hypothesis of the evil genius brutally dissociates being from thought and forces human reason to become detached from itself, to situate itself, to assure itself of its certitudes, in a word to become aware of its status within being. If it were not pushed to the limit and forced, beyond any skeptical doubt, to the "extravagant" questioning of the natural evidences of the intellect (of the type $2 + 3 = 5$), there would not be this fundamental meta-noetics that manages to establish the certitude of a first truth and of a radical foundation. The hyperbolic doubt topples and suddenly comes back as an absolute evidence. The luminous radicalism of the evidence is exactly proportionate to the hyperbolic radicalism of the *epoché* or the putting in doubt.

Metaphysics is transcended in Descartes in the direction of the radicalism of its foundations. Metaphysics is again anchored here in the this-side, in the very consciousness of the I, of the thinking subject. By going beyond the intelligible certitudes of metaphysics, by torturing reason on the scaffold of the evil genius, Descartes succeeded in bringing out the certitude of the *cogito* and of re-establishing, on the level of the act of self-consciousness, a completely new union of thought and being (*cogito ergo sum*). The "metaphysical" doubt was thus indeed a coup de force that inaugurated a new metaphysics. But this time the novelty consists in going beyond metaphysics without escaping into supertranscendence or falling back into the sensible or into lived experience. Human intelligence succeeded, by remaining on its own level, on the level of man, in transcending the natural (and up to now unfounded) evidence of its union with being, and of replacing it well on this side, in the very act by which the ego becomes conscious of its thought. Modern metaphysics opens with the *cogito* by radically banishing the support of the object and recourse to transcendence.[16] It lost both its -*physics* and its *meta-*, but intelligence gained a foundation and a "situation" in being. Metaphysics is radically transcended in a meta-noetics.

6. KANT AND THE METAPHYSICS OF METAPHYSICS

No one, however, saw more profoundly than Kant that the necessary going-beyond of metaphysics would bring us —but definitively!—from the beyond to the this-side. The Copernican revolution, which reversed the relationship between the object and the subject in knowledge, represents very clearly the transcending of the metaphysics of the object in itself towards a *metaphysics of the subject*. The critique of reason begins by questioning the most traditional assurances of human reason and attempts to show that human thought does not rest on a natural and unquestioned agreement between reason and being in itself. What was the "extravagant" hypothesis in Descartes becomes in Kant a reasoned and founded conviction. The crisis of metaphysics of the substance, which began with Locke and was continued by the criticism of the Enlightenment, was an indubitable sign that the foundations of human reason and knowledge were not self-evident, could not be self-evident.

The critique of pure reason which establishes its limits and the impossibility of metaphysics as a science could seem to be the liquidation of an age-old illusion, a simple movement of agnostic withdrawal and metaphysical temperance after the too adventurous push of classical metaphysics onto uncertain transcendental terrain. But in reality, since Kant does not purely and simply sweep away the in-itself from the philosophical scene, since he keeps it as an indispensable limit-concept or as the indispensable foundation of his "empirical realism," since he sees in the metaphysical need an intrinsic characteristic of human nature, it appears clearly that Kant does not mean simply to come back this side of the metaphysical enterprise by annulling it as an illusion, but on the contrary to preserve it by going beyond it. The Kantian critique is not situated *this side of metaphysics,* but it inaugurates, by a radical and Copernican going-beyond, *a metaphysics of the this-side.* He says so himself clearly by specifying that his critique "contains a metaphysics of metaphysics," or in other words a meta-noetics (precisely insofar as it is a critique of reason). It is a metaphysics of the subject, of self-conscious reason, of its situation and its limits.

Kant transformed the thing in itself, transcendent and separated reality—a fundamental notion of traditional metaphysics—into a structural element of reason and human knowledge. He "de-realized" the in-itself or the metaphysical as such by denying that it could be known *as independent of the mind* and by showing that human reason cannot raise itself to a plane of metaphysical reality (in the sense of an in-itself). The metaphysical is no longer the *object* of knowledge but the immanent *structure* of knowledge. The in-itself is transported into the mind as a limit-concept absolutely indispensable to the exercise and the understanding of human knowledge. This latter, instead of being the mirror or the adequate reflection of a metaphysical *reality,* will henceforth be the in-itself as a limit with its own boundaries, as that which renders consciousness of its proper limit and its situation possible, as a constitutive element *of the phenomenon.*

The metaphysics of the in-itself or of the pure intelligible is thus no longer possible; it lacks a clear consciousness of the situation of human reason and knowledge. The critique is meant to give it this consciousness. By this very fact metaphysics is transcended; we do not question its *meta-* but only its *-physics,* that is to say *its independent reality.* The in-itself, having become a structure of reason, remains transcendent but under the form of a transcendental *meta-*, which is a sort of new "transcendence" within the this-side. And the "physical" reality of this in-itself will henceforth be no more than a reality of the this-side, purely phenomenal.

Thus we can say that Kantian going-beyond consists in substituting the notion of limit for the notion of going-beyond in metaphysics. The revolution is as imposing as Plato's, but in just the opposite direction. Plato overthrew the economy of the sensible world; he exploded it by imposing on it the notion of a necessary transcending, and of a fuller reality, a "superior physics" characterized by intelligibility. By this opening up, reality toppled into the beyond. But Kant wants precisely to overthrow the economy of this intelligible world and explode now its value of reality. Reflexion, no longer on the cosmos but on reason and its foundation, imposes the notion of limit: not the common notion of limit as the cutting-off-point of the élan of knowledge, but a properly metaphysical notion of limit, as an indicator of situation, that changes all perspectives and in fact makes reality topple back into the this-side.[17]

In fact, the limit can be conceived as *indication of a beyond*, of a mysterious and unknowable transcendence that we do not penetrate: the metaphysical would be *the object of a knowledge we do not have*, that we men—given the limited or closed structure of our minds—do not possess. But Kant conceived the limit in a sense that implies a transcending of metaphysical reality in itself: as *indication of the this-side*, by which he meant that the metaphysical was *not an object of knowledge* but a structure of knowledge, precisely the limit that limits the whole *of reality* to being phenomenal, thus situated in the this-side.

The going-beyond and the progress of metaphysics can thus be summarized as follows: Traditional metaphysics lived on the admitted but still unfounded agreement between rational thought and reality (a reality independent of the mind). By learning to situate itself and to know itself, reason perceived that it had, without well-founded reasons, attributed to itself the power of rising to the level of transcendent and divine realities. Reason believed itself to be fitted for the beyond by nature or by divine right. By discovering that it is a human reason and that its domain is the this-side, it "transcends the beyond" and grasps its essential reality better. By transcending consciousness of self, reason "de-realizes" the beyond, which, however, never loses its importance as limit. Meta-noetics "de-realizes" the metaphysical. The agreement between thought and being will no longer rest on the in-itself or on a pre-established (unfounded) harmony of the intellect and the in-itself; it will rest henceforth on the transcendental that is foundation. The metaphysical foundation no longer pertains to being but to knowing; no longer to the in-itself, but to the "constitution" of the object or to the "conditions of possibility" of knowledge.

7 . HEIDEGGER AND THE DOUBLE GOING-BEYOND OF METAPHYSICS

After the decisive revolution of Kant, it would be necessary to follow the development of the new metaphysics up to the present and to specify its diverse ways of transcending. We would observe in Hegel the attempt to restore classical metaphysics on the very ground of the Kantian revolution: an attempt to elaborate a metaphysics of self-consciousness, to base a true *metaphysics of transcending* on the dialectic of the *Aufhebung,* and especially to restore the natural agreement of the rational and the real. We would then note the disdain for metaphysics among the positivists who, as we have said, revert back to this side of metaphysics by claiming to go beyond "the metaphysical stage." The influence of Kant, badly misunderstood, is balanced in the nineteenth century by the decline of metaphysics: the effort of going-beyond is no longer practiced, and scarcely even understood.

If the twentieth century opens with a renewal (Bergson, *Introduction to Metaphysics,* 1903), this is only another attempt to restore the classical metaphysics of interiority in the new garb of a philosophy of time and creation. Phenomenology at the beginning joined the camp of the anti-metaphysicians, but it quickly became apparent that Husserl's intention, especially with the introduction of the method of reduction, was oriented towards the foundation of a new ontology. Phenomenology can be justly considered as an attempt to go beyond metaphysics in the direction of a radicalization of the problem of the foundations.[18]

Heidegger belongs in this line as is shown by the *Fundamentalontologie* of *Sein und Zeit* and of *Kant und das Problem der Metaphysik,* then the lecture *Was ist Metaphysik?* and finally the recently published course of 1935: *Einführung in die Metaphysik* (1953).[19]

This ontology rests entirely on the distinction between beings (*Seinde*) and Being (*Sein*). According to Heidegger, Western philosophy has confused them too long by thinking Being in terms of the categories of beings, and by imagining that explanation by being, the traditional goal of all ontology, meant "the explanation by that being most elevated in dignity,"[20] by what was judged to be the most fundamental reality (life, matter, idea, consciousness, etc.). The question, *What is there?* was "the guiding question of metaphysics; but it is not yet the fundamental question."[21] We must now become aware of the "lack on the side of the foundations,"[22] and shift the weight of the ontological question from "that which is" to the "meaning of Being." Heidegger thus takes another step along the line we have traced up to here: he turns away from the metaphysics of essences or of objects (of beings) to return to the foundations. Now the phenomenological method renewed the problem of the foundations by attacking it through the uncovering of meanings. *Sein und Zeit* thematizes this question of the meaning of Being that had been ignored or had remained implicit in Western metaphysics. It elaborates it by unveiling this meaning from the point of view of the being which is man, from the *Dasein* and human questioning about Being finally posed as it ought to be. The enterprise of fundamental ontology is thus "to establish the foundation of metaphysics" (Grundlegung der Metaphysik).[23]

As in Kant, metaphysics is no longer self-evident and has become problematic. The question, *What is metaphysics?* is posed in such an acute manner that metaphysics, questioned by itself, undergoes its "first and most profound shock."[24] Faced with "the abyss of metaphysics,"[25] the task of the new ontology will be precisely "to uncover the internal possibility of metaphysics," "to transform the problem under consideration" in order to "preserve its authentic content."[26] Now "to preserve a problem means to liberate and safeguard the interior force which is at the source of its essence and which renders it possible as a problem."[27] We see that for Heidegger the going-beyond of metaphysics is clearly a *metaphysics of metaphysics*. Never before has it been shown so clearly that questioning (*Fragen*) and contesting are so to speak consubstantial to metaphysics itself.

If it is thus the "thematic development of our understanding of Being," i.e., uncovering of what makes possible the passage from beings to Being and founds it, we must focus essentially on the tie that binds man to Being and that is expressed as a first approximation in the very questioning about Being. Metaphysics will be "the ontological explication of the Dasein, thus of man in so far as he is, by his living understanding of Being, the place and the presence of Being."[28] Analysis of the Dasein or philosophy of the opening of the being-man to Being (*ek-sistence*) will enable us to see how Being is made explicit, that is to say how it encounters man and makes each being to be. "This is why the establishment of the foundation of metaphysics is founded on a metaphysics of the Dasein. Should we be surprised that establishing the foundation must itself certainly and even eminently be a metaphysics?"[29]

However, we see from his more recent writings that Heidegger did not stop there.[30] His going-beyond was so abrupt and decisive that language would not long support such a distortion of the term metaphysics. How would it be possible to designate with one term traditional metaphysics and this new "metaphysics?" The going-beyond tended to become a liquidation: either one or the other! It is very significant that, by proclaiming now the necessity of an *Überwindung der Metaphysik,*[31] Heidegger goes beyond metaphysics in a different meaning of the expression go-beyond from that used in the course of this article. He opts for its liquidation. He reserves the meaning of the word "metaphysics" for a past state, "transcended," in his eyes completed. He discredits it because it must make way for something very different from what the metaphysicians since Plato have aimed at.

"It is now a question of clearing a passage from metaphysics to the thought of the truth of Being."[32] This will no longer be even a fundamental ontology but a new *thinking* (*Denken*), a thinking that is "more thinking," a "thinking to come": "the thinking of Being."[33] This is no longer

an internal questioning of metaphysics by itself, but a con-
demnation. Metaphysics is no longer a problem to itself; it
is banished.[34] Anxious to show the unity of his purpose,
Heidegger certainly would categorically refuse to distinguish two steps in his evolution. We do not wish to assert
that he is wrong if by that he means that his ontological
intention, or the meaning of his "break-through," is the
same in 1927 and in 1950 and that the continuity is perfect.
But it is no less true that what was the establishment of the
foundation of metaphysics has now become an adieu to
metaphysics.

Heidegger's aim is no longer to clear a path from anthropology to Being. Today he wants to comprehend human thought or the possibility of man's questioning about
Being by an opposite approach: by beginning with Being
(or the *Wahrheit des Seins*) which reveals itself, opens itself and speaks first. The problem of the *foundation*
(*Grund*) which was originally posed from the Dasein, is
now posed from the side of Being. This is to say that *it is no
longer a "problem"* or a question, the object of a human
Fragen. It is an "advent" or a "happening," a sort of
"grace"; it is what renders human questioning in general
possible.

Hence ontological questioning, which went from beings to Being and which seemed, under that title, already
revolutionary, was only a provisional break, still completely conditioned by what it wanted to transcend. The
metaphysics that we thought we found in the fundamental
ontology of *Sein und Zeit* was not what Heidegger means
today. It was still too much obscured by the centuries-old
confusion between Being and beings, because it still
thought it was necessary to go from beings towards their
foundation which would be Being. It imagined that its task
was, as in the past, a search for the foundations, meta-

physics having always in fact believed, by an ineradicable atavism, that it had to "express Being."[35]

Thus metaphysics was an "unconscious barrier."[36] The distinction between Being and beings should not have been understood (Heidegger now tells us) as a distinction interior to metaphysics; it was not a deeper search for the foundations (what we have up to now understood by "going beyond metaphysics"). It was the indication of a rupture with metaphysics, for, like man in Nietzsche, it is something to *überwinden,* to get over, if one wants truly to be attentive to Being, Being which has to speak and transmit "by its silent voice" a message that has never been expressed to this day. The truth of Being is an "unfounded, unknown foundation,"[37] but not in the "metaphysical" sense. It is necessary that man learn "not to think metaphysically any more."[38] "The thought which comes is no longer philosophy because it thinks more originally than metaphysics."[39]

It is a question of "going back to the foundation of metaphysics."[40] But this is a completely different thing from establishing its foundation because *we cannot go back "by starting from metaphysics."* By following the modes of metaphysical thought, philosophy has continued during the course of centuries to abandon its *Grund* and to forget Being in order to hypnotize itself with beings.[41] In order to rediscover this *Grund* which is the truth of Being, it is necessary to leave the domain of ontology where the metaphysician speaks (*logos*) about beings (*onta*). It is necessary to surmount the obstacle of metaphysics.[42]

But, if this is the case, if Being is nothingness and foundation, if it speaks first and if man must efface himself before it, then human intelligence is no longer a problem. To this unquestioned intelligence there inescapably corresponds a sort of absolute thought: the effort of the

"thinker" does not tend so much to think as to be silent or
to "let itself be thought by Being," so to speak. It is Being
that founds thought: the only question is to open and to be
opened. But is a philosophy of *openness* still philosophy, or
is it revelation? In any case, it is no longer metaphysics.

If the first going-beyond established a metaphysics and
the second excludes it, we cannot, in spite of the protests
of the author, interpret the first approach in function of
the second[43] and refuse the second precisely in the name of
the first. It is rather improbable that the later Heidegger
will be called upon to fecundate philosophical thought to
the extent that the early Heidegger did. And if the distinction of Being from beings should lead finally to the dis-
crediting of metaphysics, it is because Heidegger did not
succeed in incorporating in it the substance of the Western
metaphysical tradition. Rejected or forgotten history takes
its revenge as much as, if not more than, the forgetfulness of
Being. In reality, neither the meta-metaphysics, nor the
metaphysics of interiority or of the act, nor the metaphysics
of the *cogito,* nor that of Kant was oriented towards beings.
Unfortunately, Heidegger has not rendered justice to all
these attempts. He has chosen to dismiss them as concerned
only with beings—in which he sees an ancient illusion as
well as an obstacle that is all too present. He would charge
metaphysics with the responsibility for a serious forgetfulness (that of Being) in which the destiny of Western
civilization is involved.

But what do we see? The philosopher who today incon-
testably possesses the genius for metaphysical *Fragen* in the
highest degree and who therefore has renewed the problem
of the foundations, the philosopher who appears as the
most radical of the metaphysicians, practically and in fact
rejoins with his conception of the *Überwindung der Metaphysik* the position of the anti-metaphysical positivists,[44] or

that of Nietzsche, so strongly impregnated with evolutionist positivism and so hostile to the philosophies of other-worlds. As for the positivists, metaphysics is an historical stage which certainly had its *raison d'être,* but which now appears as the major hindrance, the principal obstacle to be thrust aside in order to clear the path to the essential. As for the positivists, the destiny of civilization is at stake. We find again the same pathos of the decisive moment of historical evolution at which, thanks to a man (it was Comte, it is Heidegger), an essential revelation for the destiny of humanity and civilization can at last be manifested. Already Heidegger, in the role of *Denker* (in the strong and anti-metaphysical sense he gives this word), is *nolens volens* the high-priest of this revelation,[45] as Comte was of the religion of Humanity. He *has to* speak henceforth in oracles or be still.

It would be impossible to say exactly whether the *Überwindung der Metaphysik* here rejoins the neo-platonic tradition of meta-metaphysics—so strong in the German philosophical tradition from Meister Eckhart up to the postkantians and even to Jaspers—or whether it rather finally falls back below the level of metaphysics: not of course, like the positivists, to the level of experimentation and scientific verification, but to the level of a quasi-ineffable experience of Being and its truth. Perhaps the distance between these two experiences is not ultimately so great as it appears.

CONCLUSION

Understood in the movement of its perpetual transcendings, metaphysics thus appears to us as an élan of questioning rather than as immobilization in a system. And from this fact one has the right to conclude to a progressive deepening of the metaphysical problem: at each going-beyond, a whole block of unfounded certitudes, a whole order of dogmatic evidences is put in question and submitted to the trial of criticism. What was self-evident becomes successively problematic. The *physis* and the changing here-below were the first problem and it seemed that metaphysics oriented itself towards the beyond and the absolute and that there it would find definitive certainty. But the evidences of the beyond, in their turn, became problematic when the intellect began to reflect on its origin and its own foundations. Finally, metaphysics became more and more problematic in its own eyes.

However, in distinction from skeptical doubt and suspension of judgment (always joined to a metaphysics of the object in itself), these contestations and questionings do not signify that one despairs of finding truth. Rather, one becomes more demanding and more ardent in one's search. One becomes aware that if unfounded certitude becomes a problem, this does not necessarily mean that it is erroneous; it simply means that it is not yet sufficiently true. That is why metaphysical questioning turns more and more from absolute reality towards the first foundation, passes from being to knowing, from ontology to critique and even to anthropology. At each step we are taken a little more this side: from the object to the subject, from being to the intellect, from the physical to the noetic, from the heaven of other-worlds to earth, from the divine to the human.

Formerly the metaphysician climbed up the ladder of being, sought for the unchanging, considered the world *sub specie aeternitatis*. Today he "meets being on this side of the phenomenon,"[46] he attaches himself to the foundation, to meaning, to the temporal and to the situation of man in the *hic et nunc;* and he tries to rediscover the object in this new light.

If metaphysics is questioning, does this mean that it is an enterprise of demolishing our most vital certitudes? Fine result if ultimately, as it may seem, neither the certitudes of the this-side, nor those of the beyond, nor finally those of reason resist critical questioning and if everything is condemned to be perpetually put in question again. In that case what is the meaning of this search for the foundations which succeeds only in breaking down certitudes and in cutting off one by one the branches on which man is sitting? Is this still metaphysics?

This return to the this-side, we have seen, is not a jaded withdrawal or a less vigilant abandonment to the mirages of subjectivity. Human reason had tried to go beyond itself, to open up for itself a dimension of transcendence first of all on the level of a reality which it contemplated and in which it distinguished a this-side and a beyond. It is as if it had first to exercise itself somehow on the level of an object with a certain distension. This distance which the metaphysician dug out between the real and the apparent, between light and shadow, transcendence and the here-below, mimicked in advance the distension to which reason had to subject itself and by which it went beyond the first dimension of transcendence by giving it its most profound meaning. Detaching itself now from its own proper evidence, it instituted within itself a kind of new relationship between the founded and the non-founded; it took its distance and became aware little by little that this rent which suddenly made it a stranger in its own eyes, this gap which forced it to become ex-centric to itself and to seek itself without ceasing, was an internal distension or the opening up of a dimension of self-consciousness. Reason thus discovered a relationship to itself which alone could constitute it and found it as reason. Not the anxious return to itself of a subjectivity too much preoccupied with itself, but rather a manner of liberating itself from itself, a new relationship, more detached, more disinterested, more authentic, that the self could maintain with itself and which was entirely directed towards an objectivity more unpreoccupied with itself and towards a new recapturing of the world of objects. To conquer the unawareness of self which characterizes reason when it thinks itself to be unquestioned or the trustee of the secret of things, to conquer the ignorance of self, such has been the ambition of philosophy since Socrates. The Sophist was full of himself, even when he spoke of things. Socrates established a dis-equilibrated relationship with himself, even if—and precisely because—he tried to know himself.

This relationship to self is essentially metaphysical because of the questioning which gives it birth and because of the distance it introduces at the heart of the real. Certainly the meta- of metaphysics no longer indicates "spatial" transcendence towards a beyond or movement to the absolute. It indicates a transmutation within consciousness, a transcending of self that is much rather a dis-absolutization of consciousness or, as Sartre says, a way of decompressing its thickness. Reason, instead of simply being self, full of its evidences, becomes relationship to self, consciousness of self. This relationship marks its non-coincidence with itself, and the questioning which renders it a problem to itself awakens its consciousness of situation. A reason which feels itself questioned—by itself—no longer escapes towards absolutes, no longer takes itself for divine. Metaphysics is no longer a pretext for it to divinize itself. Its questioning is precisely an indication of the this-side; it is incessant creation and re-creation of a distance which no longer needs to be annulled because it is the valid acquisition of a more acute consciousness. A reason which would coincide with itself (mankind's ancient dream) would be bundled up in its own absoluteness and would justly expose itself to the raillery of anti-metaphysicians and skeptics. It would have succumbed to the glamour of retreat into unconsciousness (of an unconsciousness that can also be "metaphysical"). It would have installed itself in the truth, but this would no longer be really more than *its* truth. A possessed truth is a subjective truth, at least from one side. But the true truth is metaphysical. This means first of all that one does not possess it but, as Plato said, one loves it, and it is this that makes one more a philosopher than a sage. This also means that one does not approach it except by a questioning of self, by blowing up one's illusory autarchy, by opening up consciousness of self, in short by this internal transcendence to the this-side which is, within the human condition, the only authentic break-through safe from the temptations of flight.

Meta-noetics is thus faithful to the most fundamental aim of metaphysics. It is the necessary transcending of metaphysics in the direction of consciousness. Metaphysics also is detached from itself and acquires an awareness of its situation which it did not have previously. And it is no simple play on words if we like to speak today of "the metaphysics of metaphysics,"[47] of "the philosophy of philosophy,"[48] of "the phenomenology of phenomenology,"[49] or of "the dialectic of dialectics."[50] The doubling is not an "elevation" to a power, but the "descent into the pit" of consciousness of self in which Kant saw "the only path of apotheosis," the return down into the Cave, or a more profound reflexion.

If, from this perspective, our world, our human life, our reason, and our metaphysics become more fragile and more precarious, do not the solid ulterior-worlds of former

times, by comparison, also become more true, more authentic, more worthy of being experienced? —Or is it necessary to think that metaphysics interests us only to the
extent that it dispenses us from *taking the responsibility
for truth,* that it reopens for us with one turn of the key the
doors of a lost paradise, momentarily closed? If we felt that
the purpose of metaphysics was to give man a balm for his
pain and a route of escape, we would be the first to say that
it is necessary to go beyond metaphysics by liquidating it.
But since through the centuries it has always been the
instrument for sharpening our consciousness as men, we
will not abandon it. We will follow the going-beyond
which it points out to us whenever it enables us to become
more clearly and distinctly conscious of our human condition.

NOTES

INTRODUCTION

1. See the bibliography at the end of this volume.

2. The first of these essays, "Qu'est-ce que la phénoménologie?" was originally published in the *Revue de Théologie et de Philosophie* in three installments in 1952 (pp. 7–30, 126–140, 294–316). The second essay, "La question du point de départ radical chez Descartes et Husserl," originally appeared in *Problèmes actuels de la phénoménologie* (Actes du Colloque international de phénoménologie, Bruxelles, avril, 1951), Paris, 1952, pp. 9–30. The third essay, "Réflexion et conscience de soi," originally appeared in the *Tijdschrift voor Philosophie,* 1953, pp. 440–456. And the final essay, "Le dépassement de la métaphysique," originally appeared in the *Revue internationale de philosophie,* 1954, pp. 189–217. The last three essays were reprinted in *L'Homme et sa raison,* 2 vols., Neuchâtel, 1956.

3. Herbert Spiegelberg listed the article "Qu'est-ce que la phénoménologie?" as "one of the best historical and critical introductions to both the German and French phases of the Phenomenological Movement" and placed it on his list of *desiderata* for immediate publication in English (*The Phenomenological Movement,* II, 591, 648).

4. Pierre Thévenaz was born in 1913 at Neuchâtel in Switzerland and died there in 1955. After his death his writings were collected and edited by Paul Ricoeur in two volumes under the title, *L'homme et sa raison.* For these volumes Ricoeur wrote a valuable preface entitled "Pierre Thévenaz, Un philosophe protestant," pp. 9–26. Thévenaz died at the untimely age of 42, before he was able to do more than begin his projected life's work of writing a "Protestant philosophy." If this aim appears somewhat singular at first sight, it becomes less so when Thévenaz is situated within the French personalist tradition. His close personal friendship with Emmanuel

Mounier, the Roman Catholic editor of *Esprit* and founder of the Catholic personalist movement in France, is enough to indicate that Thévenaz did not philosophize in a closed or partisan manner. For him the phrase "Protestant philosophy" was another way—a post-Reformation way—of saying "Christian philosophy," by which he did not mean an attempt to arrive at ecclesiastical dogma through philosophy, but a freeing of man, after the death of the "God of the philosophers" and after the end of "philosophical theology," to philosophize "without an absolute." It is not, in his view, the place of philosophy to speak "about" God, much less to speak from the point of view of God, but only to speak with a feeling of responsibility *before God* (Ricoeur, pp. 10–11). In any case, this aspect of Thévenaz' thought is without bearing on the purpose of this volume.

5. Cf. particularly two essays not included in this selection: "La philosophie sans absolu," *L'homme et sa raison,* I, 187–206, and "Les révolutions philosophiques du XXe siècle," *ibid.,* II, 99–120.

6. Maurice Merleau-Ponty, *Phénoménologie de la perception,* Paris, 1954, p. i. A discussion of four "antinomies" of phenomenology follows immediately after this quotation.

7. This helps explain how it is possible for even the most acute adherents of Oxfordian linguistic analysis to write on questions which entail a theory of perception, a theory of consciousness (mind) and a theory of action, without so much as a glance in the direction of continental philosophers preoccupied with the same questions, and in many cases arguing similar positions. This explains, for instance, how Stuart Hampshire in his admirable book, *Thought and Action,* London, 1959, is able to treat at length such notions as "intention" and even the "intentionality" of consciousness (mind) without ever taking into consideration the much more advanced studies on this subject in Husserl, Merleau-Ponty, and other phenomenologists. Hampshire never really gets beyond an Aristotelian conception of "intentionality" (as intentional behavior), though, within this framework, he reaches conclusions of great value and originality. Hampshire sometimes gives the impression of being "un phénoménologue manqué."

8. "The most important event in philosophy before the War was certainly the appearance of . . . the first volume of Husserl's major work." Sartre, *Imagination,* Paris, 1948, p. 139.

9. Dorian Cairns, "Phenomenology," in Vergilius Ferm, *A History of Philosophical Systems,* New York, 1950, p. 363. Herbert Spiegelberg also notes that the hold of phenomenology in America is at the present time "tenuous," at least in philosophy. It is through psychology, psychiatry, and religion that the phenomenological method has

gained its first solid foothold in American thought (*The Phenomeno-logical Movement*, II, 637).

10. A cross section would find such diverse thinkers as Walter Kaufmann (*Critique of Philosophy and Religion*, New York, 1958), Maurice Natanson ("Phenomenology and the Natural Attitude," *Journal of Philosophy*, November 19, 1959) and Morton White (*Age of Analysis*, Mentor, 1955) in agreement on this point. To quote only the last-named, Morton White calls for "courageous souls" to "penetrate the thick fog that has dropped between . . . philosophers of the continent and . . . English-speaking philosophers," and thus lay the basis for a greater rapprochement and mutual enrichment (p. 238). It is unfortunate that in this same book he allows himself "an excusable amount of irony" (p. 242) in presenting points of view for which he has no sympathy and which, on his own admission, he does not understand. His treatment of Husserl (pp. 100–104) is one of the most astonishing chapters in contemporary pocketbook philosophy. Since he cannot "understand [Husserl] well enough to expound" even the central features of his thought, one wonders what could have induced him to try.

11. It is interesting to note that nearly all the reviews devoted to Heidegger in British and American philosophical journals dismiss his entire enterprise with the accusation that he has not studied formal logic! (For a recent example, cf. Walter Cerf in *Philosophy and Phenomenological Research*, September, 1961, pp. 109–112). The treatment usually given to Sartre seems to have a more emotional basis. People, particularly English philosophers, simply don't *have* the experiences which for a Sartre, a Malraux, a Camus, or a Dostoevsky are paradigm cases. One suspects, in reading the frequent Anglo-American accusations of "muddled logic" leveled against Sartre, that their authors are really distressed by so much empirical experience. But a philosophy rooted in experience and directed towards the analysis of experience, rather than towards talk about experience, is impervious to "logical" vivisection in the manner in which it is currently practiced in England and America.

12. One cannot help but think of William James in this connection. In his day American thought *did* furnish the philosophical bridge across the Channel. (Here again we are in agreement with Morton White, *op. cit.*, p. 174.) It is possible to show, though this must wait for full treatment in a later study, that James' most profound contributions to philosophy give American pragmatism the means of extending its research in a phenomenological direction and of incorporating many of the discoveries and advances of continental philosophers, particularly in philosophical anthropology and the theory of consciousness.

13. Contrary to what many have thought, Husserl's cryptic statement towards the end of his life—"Philosophy as a rigorous science . . . the dream is over"—is not to be taken as a renunciation of this ideal. (In this connection, cf. Q. Lauer, introduction to *La Philosophie comme science rigoureuse,* Paris, 1955, p. 7, and Herbert Spiegelberg, *op. cit.,* p. 77, n. 2.)

14. *Philosophie als strenge Wissenschaft,* p. 340, *Ideen,* No. 20.

15. *Nachwort zu meinen Ideen,* p. 14.

16. Eugen Fink's expression, approved by Husserl.

17. We have used the term *structure* of experience ("structure" of consciousness, noetic-noematic "structure") because it better expresses the aim of phenomenological research in its generality; by speaking in this way we can better show the unity of the phenomenological method common to Husserl, Heidegger, Sartre, and Merleau-Ponty. Husserl's more usual term was *eidos* ("eidetic definition") or *essence (Wesen).* But note that the Husserlian "essence" is not a clear and distinct idea; it is not really a "what." It is a "non-fixed," "asymtotic," "morphological" *eidos,* which is revealed as the structure of experience through the phenomenological analysis of the noetic act and its noematic correlate in any given experience (whether perceptive, imaginative, emotive, categorial, etc.).

18. Kierkegaard, *Fear and Trembling,* Anchor, pp. 22–23.

19. Lucie Gilson, *La psychologie descriptive selon Franz Brentano,* Paris, 1955, pp. 63–64 and *passim.* Cf. also *id., Méthode et métaphysique selon Franz Brentano,* Paris, 1955, *passim.*

20. Husserl frequently speaks of Descartes as his predecessor, especially in the *Cartesian Meditations.* Cf. André de Muralt, *L'idée de la phénoménologie,* Paris, 1958, p. 103 and *passim.*

21. On this question Gilbert Ryle (*The Concept of Mind,* 1949) and Merleau-Ponty (*Phénoménologie de la perception,* 1945) could find themselves in surprising accord. Both are philosophers of human behavior; both attempt to establish the basis for a non-dualistic "behaviorism." But it would be dangerous to press their agreement further. It is noteworthy that while British empiricism successfully resisted Cartesianism and reflexive analysis in the French manner (which is considered by Thévenaz to be the really profound and important contribution of Descartes), they were no match for Cartesian dualism. In fact, it must be said that British empiricism has prolonged the "metaphysical" life of body-mind dualism down to the present day—long after it had been weakened and even abandoned on the continent. One can only applaud the present tendency in British philosophy to abandon this outmoded "empiricist" theory of mind. But without elaborating a truly unitary theory of man and thus getting beneath the fully reflexive *cogito,* it is questionable to

what extent British philosophy will be able to overcome this "here-dodegenerative defect" which it has handed down from generation to generation since the time of Locke. (Cf. Erwin Straus, "Aesthesiology and Hallucinations" in *Existence,* New York, 1958, p. 149.)

22. A. J. Ayer in his book *Language, Truth and Logic,* 1946, after defining philosophy as nothing but purely formal analysis, sets out to give us examples of philosophers of the past who were primarily "analytical" and therefore "philosophical." In this way he tries to save *some* of the past history of philosophy from oblivion. "I think it can be shown," he writes, "that the majority of those who are commonly supposed to have been great philosophers were primarily not metaphysicians but analysts" (Dover ed., p. 52). We are not really surprised to find that the list of those "great philosophers" who partially understood what philosophy is consists almost exclusively of British empiricists. Thévenaz' essay on "Going Beyond Meta-physics" in this volume is a useful antidote to such philosophical im-perialism. If we define philosophy, phenomenologically, as a meta-physics of experience, we get a list of "greats" (Plotinus, Augustine, Descartes, Kant, Bergson, Husserl, James) which it is very doubtful Ayer would accept as philosophers at all. This illustrates one of the most profound differences between phenomenology and analytical philosophy: the former takes the "historicity" of experience (and hence of the philosophical effort of Western man) seriously, as a philosophical problem; the latter is a-historical if not anti-historical, a philosophy of the disembodied *cogito.*

23. Cf. J.-P. Sartre, *The Transcendence of the Ego,* ed. Williams and Kirkpatrick, pp. 43 ff.

24. For a more developed discussion of this question, cf. John Wild, *The Challenge of Existentialism,* Indiana University Press, 1959, pp. 90–95 and *passim.*

25. In phrasing the problematic of phenomenology in this way, we must not forget that the life-world is strictly correlative to constitut-ing consciousness. Again, phenomenology does not study the object of consciousness nor the act of consciousness in isolation from one another, but the very structure of their strict correlativity in experi-ence.

26. Certain characteristics of Heidegger's method of teaching, his intensity, the restriction of his company to a small circle of intimate disciples, his habit of speaking aphoristically, and the consequent worshipful attitude of some members of his coterie are not without parallel in the lives of other German philosophers of the recent past who have, for all that, received favorable treatment at the hands of Englishmen. Cf. Norman Malcolm, *Ludwig Wittgenstein, A Memoir,* London, 1958, *passim.* If Heidegger has earned his title as "The

Magician of Freiburg," and if he sometimes seems to act like a kind of twentieth-century Paracelsus, it is still not evident that this constitutes *ipso facto* a refutation of his thought.

27. Maurice Merleau-Ponty, "Sur la phénoménologie du langage," *Signes,* Paris, 1960, pp. 105 ff. Cf. also *Phénoménologie de la perception,* Part I, chapter 6.

28. This "before" does not necessarily imply *temporal* priority. As an example of a non-illuminating because non-irreducible distinction which still seems to have considerable prestige in the analytical philosophy of language, but which is phenomenologically useless, we can take Carnap's distinction (*Philosophy and Logical Syntax,* 1935) between the "expressive function" and the "representative function" of language. Precisely because the "representative function" (if it makes sense to say that language is "representative") is also expressive, and secondarily derived from "expression," this distinction remains on the surface of language-analysis and misses the fact that actual "expression" cannot usefully be divided into such non-essential (non-eidetic) classifications, at least as far as phenomenology is concerned.

29. But William Barrett has pointed this out (*Irrational Man,* New York, 1958, pp. 16–17). Cf. also Geoffrey Clive, *The Romantic Enlightenment,* New York, 1960, chapter 3. Aron Gurwitsch in his recent book, *Théorie du champ de la conscience,* Paris, 1957, deals at length with William James' contribution to the phenomenological theory of consciousness.

30. However, the thought of William James *did* have a direct influence on Husserl (cf. Spiegelberg, *The Phenomenological Movement,* I, 111–117), and Sartre has also called attention to the importance of James' psychology. A very recent book by Johannes Linschoten attests to the continuing interest in James' thought on the continent (*Auf dem Wege zu einer phänomenologischen Psychologie, Die Psychologie von William James,* Berlin, 1961).

31. As an example, one of the typical irrelevancies of pragmatist "logicians" consists of attempting to reduce the "lived-subjunctive" and the "lived-optative" to hypothetical if-then propositions, as if lived "could-would" experiences (and the like) could be simply translated into symbolic representation while retaining their *meaning.* They can be so translated, but only by an impoverishment of their existential and empirical meaning so great as to render such procedures practically useless in the clarification of experience. The impossibility of "schematizing" experience with a few abstract, logical devices is probably the main reason why pragmatism as a philosophy of experience has been on the wane almost since the death of

James himself. Again, the substantiation of such a charge here would take us too far afield and must be left to a later study.

WHAT IS PHENOMENOLOGY?

1. However, if the *Deux Sources* (1932) are the logical outcome, in the realm of ethics and religion, of the discoveries of the *Essai* (1889) and do not require any essential modification of Bergsonism, it is not possible to say the same for Husserl. The *Krisis* (1936) is not simply the development of the *Logische Untersuchungen* (1900).

2. G. Lehmann (*Die deutsche Philosophie der Gegenwart,* Stuttgart, 1943) has no chapter on Husserl (but gives an entire chapter to Rosenberg!) and tries to explain the phenomenological philosophy of Aryans like Scheler or Heidegger by a sort of spontaneous generation, or by attaching them directly to the nineteenth century. The name of Husserl is hardly cited; he is cavalierly and scandalously "liquidated" as an obscure Jewish mystic (!) to whom, as to Spinoza, some have attributed a philosophical importance that he does not have.

3. Thus the critique of psychologism and relativism in Volume I of the *Logische Untersuchungen* cannot be properly understood except in the light of the analyses of intentionality in Volume II; then, the whole of the *Logische Untersuchungen,* in the light of the transcendental viewpoint of the *Ideen;* finally, the "residual" consciousness of the reduction (in the *Ideen*), in the light of the phenomenology of the constituting activity (*Leistung*) of the later works, etc.

4. This is the way Husserl himself characterizes his progress in the *Logische Untersuchungen,* p. 17, and in the *Krisis,* p. 133.

5. *Die Idee der Phänomenologie, Husserliana,* II, 19.

6. *Ibid.,* p. ix: "Wesenslehre der Erkenntnis."

7. *Ibid.,* p. 6.

8. *Méditations cartésiennes,* p. 28.

9. *Ibid.,* p. 27.

10. Thus, if Husserl in the *Logische Untersuchungen* isolates ideal realities, meanings susceptible of a phenomenological description, let us not commit the error, so often committed, of seeing there some kind of Platonic realism.

11. We can illustrate this point by recalling the new relation that Husserl conceives between science and philosophy, a question which is decisive for his problem of the radical foundation. From the time of his discovery of the phenomenological reduction (1905–1907) his position remains unchanged: on the one hand, like Descartes, he is convinced of the unity of reason (and thus of science and philosophy in a *mathesis universalis*); he is likewise convinced that philosophy must be a "rigorous science"; but, on the other hand, he recognizes

that the problem of a radical foundation of reason (which is not simply the problem of the foundations of science or the sciences) requires, as an essential condition of its solution, a radical distinction between science and philosophy. The reduction no longer traces the break between the rational disciplines (philosophy and science) and natural knowledge, but between (transcendental, non-mundane) philosophy and science regarded as belonging to the natural world. Even philosophers like Descartes and Kant remained caught in the natural attitude. The originality of Husserlian transcendentalism lies in a new sort of *distance* taken with respect to science as the content of knowledge, in a deliberate break with the natural attitude of the scientist, in order the better to rediscover, thanks to the reduction, the implicit intention and meaning of science, in an essential *proximity* to it that no epistemology, not even positivist or scientist, has ever known.

12. *Die Idee der Phänomenologie*, pp. 25–26.

13. *Ibid.*, p. 90.

14. *Journal*, September 25, 1906, cited by W. Biemel in his introduction to *Die Idee der Phänomenologie*, p. vii.

15. As in the case of Bergsonian intuition, it is an immediate *reflexive* seeing and not the simple seeing of immediate perception; it is also a creative intuition, a seeing that is at the same time a willing and an acting.

16. The expression is found in a marginal note in *Ideen I, Husserliana*, III, 463.

17. According to the expression of Eugen Fink.

18. "Philosophie als strenge Wissenschaft," *Logos*, I, 1911.

19. In fact, towards the end of his life he wrote in his journal: "Philosophy as a rigorous science, the dream is over." This significant sentence is cited in a recent and very instructive article (with which I was not yet acquainted when I wrote my first article) by A. De Waelhens, "Husserl et la phénoménologie," *Critique*, 1951, pp. 1044–1057. There De Waelhens raises the important problems of Husserl's later philosophy and of post-husserlian phenomenology: the lived world (*Lebenswelt*), the ontological status of the subject and perception, "one of the keys of phenomenology."

On the relations between phenomenology and Hegel on the one side and Marx on the other, we can add likewise a study by A. De Waelhens, "Phénoménologie et dialectique," in *Ordre, Désordre, Lumière* (Collège philosophique), Paris, 1952, pp. 9–31, and a review by the same author of the book by Tran-Duc-Thao in *Critique*, 1952, pp. 85–88.

On the relations between Husserl and post-husserlian phenomenology see *Problèmes actuels de la phénoménologie* (Actes du Colloque international de phénoménologie de Bruxelles, 1951), Paris, 1952, and Ludwig Landgrebe, *Phänomenologie und Metaphysik,* Hamburg, 1949.

20. His doctoral thesis was devoted to the theory of signification in Duns Scotus.

21. *Sein und Zeit,* p. 35.

22. Heidegger belongs to the second generation of Husserl's disciples and his philosophy is tributary to transcendental phenomenology.

23. *Sein und Zeit,* pp. 5, 41.

24. One of his recent texts is entitled "The Going Back to the Foundation of Metaphysics" (Rückgang in den Grund der Metaphysik) and serves as the introduction to the last edition of *Was ist Metaphysik?* (1951).

25. *Was ist Metaphysik?* 1951, p. 19.

26. *"Grund des Grundes." Vom Wesen des Grundes,* 1949, p. 49.

27. Cf. *Was ist Metaphysik?* This is also the direction in which Sartre will develop Heidegger's thought.

28. According to the expression of J. Wahl, "Essai sur le néant d'un problème," *Deucalion,* I, 1946, p. 44.

29. It remains, nevertheless, that the enormous influence of Heidegger in philosophy, in theology, in psychology, and in psychiatry during the past quarter-century has been exercised on the anthropological and existentiel level that Heidegger himself explicitly rejects. It is doubtful that the "true" philosophy of Heidegger, which he is now developing (see below) and of which he gives the official interpretation, will ever exercise a comparable influence, except perhaps in the area of the philosophy of language, aesthetics, and literary analysis.

30. *Le Concept de Monde chez Heidegger,* Louvain, 1950, p. 81.

31. *Vom Wesen der Wahrheit,* p. 16 (*De l'essence de la vérité,* p. 85).

32. Cited by Biemel, *Concept . . . ,* p. 81.

33. This neologism (existentiel-existential) is meant to mark this change of level.

34. A. De Waelhens, *La philosophie de Martin Heidegger,* Louvain, 1942, pp. 7–8.

35. *Vom Wesen der Wahrheit* (1943), *Erläuterungen zu Hölderlins Dichtung* (1944), *Über den Humanismus* (1947), *Holzwege* (1950), *Was ist Metaphysik?* (1951).

36. As the recent book by Egon Vietta, *Die Seinsfrage bei Martin Heidegger,* Stuttgart, 1950, bears witness.

37. *Über den Humanismus,* 1947, p. 57 and *passim;* Vietta, *op. cit.,* pp. 40, 59.

38. We find this in Husserl in the *Logische Untersuchungen,* in Sartre, and especially in Merleau-Ponty. We will come back to this.

39. In the line of such a phenomenology of language we find H. Schmalenbach, "Phénoménologie du signe," *Signe et symbole,* (Être et Penser, No. 13), Neuchâtel, 1946, pp. 49–103.

40. From an unpublished course on Hölderlin cited by Vietta, *op. cit.,* p. 74.

41. *Was ist Metaphysik?* 1951, p. 46.

42. *Über den Humanismus,* 1947, p. 116.

43. *Ibid.,* p. 60.

44. *"Das Nennen des Dichters, das Sagen des Denkers." Was ist Metaphysik?* p. 46.

45. *Vom Wesen der Wahrheit,* p. 28; *Was ist Metaphysik?* 1951, p. 39.

46. *Was ist Metaphysik?* p. 19.

47. *Ibid.,* p. 8.

48. *Ibid.,* p. 12.

49. *"Gesagter." Über den Humanismus,* 1947, p. 84.

50. Cf. *ibid.,* p. 55.

51. *Über den Humanismus,* p. 119.

52. *Ibid.,* pp. 60–61.

53. "Heimkunft," according to the title of the elegy of Hölderlin interpreted by Heidegger. See also *Über den Humanismus,* p. 84. We rediscover here the Platonic and Plotinian theme of the return to the lost "fatherland": *Theatetus* 176 a–b, Plotinus, *Enneads,* I, 6, 8.

54. *Über den Humanismus,* p. 85.

55. *Sein und Zeit,* p. 173.

56. *Über den Humanismus,* p. 90.

57. *Ibid.*

58. *Ibid.,* p. 53. Cf. the note of R. Savioz in *Revue de Théologie et de Philosophie,* 1951, pp. 297–300.

59. *Über den Humanismus,* p. 84.

60. Vietta, *op. cit.,* p. 88: "es" fragt im Menschen. —Only let us remark, "it" does not question all alone; the thinker and the poet are the mediators or the prophets, almost sacred figures. Unhappily, Heidegger is not far from considering himself the high priest of a new religion of mysteries or initiation. Many passages testify to the disquieting pride that such an attitude carries with it. If "in *Sein und Zeit* the decisive call of destiny to thought" (*der geschickhafte Anspruch an das Denken*) has remained without an echo, if "philosophy with the self-assurance of a sleep-walker has passed by the true and unique question of *Sein und Zeit,*" "it is not because of misunderstandings with regard to a book but because of our desertion of Being" (*Was ist Metaphysik?* p. 17). Or again: "*Sein und Zeit* is

neither an ideal, nor a program, but the first beginning in which the actualization (*Wesung, "esséification"*) of Being itself is prepared" (an unpublished text cited by Vietta, *op. cit.*, p. 130). That such an attitude is capable in present-day Germany of fascinating even philosophers of worth, Vietta's whole book, alas, bears but too eloquent witness! These Heideggerians who denounce with scorn the philistine and quixotic spirit of the Herren Professoren offer us—or rather reserve to themselves—an esoteric doctrine that certainly is worth even less and which cannot fail to sterilize philosophy quickly. Decidedly, we part ways with phenomenology and we no longer recognize in this new dogmatism the spirit of honest, patient, and modest research that animated the thought of Husserl.

61. It is significant that it is a long time since Heidegger has claimed the phenomenological method and that there is no trace of the word phenomenology in his most recent writings.

62. *Über den Humanismus,* p. 80.

63. *Ibid.,* p. 102.

64. *Ibid.,* p. 76. Cf. the note of R. Savioz, cited above, p. 300.

65. *Über den Humanismus,* p. 76.

66. *Ibid.,* p. 101.

67. *Ibid.,* p. 102.

68. *Ibid.*

69. "Il sentiero," Italian translation in *Il Solipsismo,* (Archivio di Filosofia), Padua, 1950, p. 19.

70. In the text Heidegger plays on the French words *"avènement"* and *"avenant," Über den Humanismus,* p. 117.

71. Cf. A. De Waelhens, "De la phénoménologie à l'existentialisme," in *Le Choix, le Monde, l'Existence,* Grenoble-Paris, 1948, pp. 37–82, and "Heidegger et Sartre," in *Deucalion* I, Paris, 1946, pp. 13–37. See also Gilbert Varet, *L'ontologie de Sartre,* Paris, 1948, which is the most penetrating critique which has been written on the *philosophy* of Sartre; and Jean Wahl, "Essai sur le néant d'un problème," *Deucalion* I, pp. 41–72, and "Sur l'introduction à l'Être et le Néant," *Deucalion* 3, Neuchâtel, 1950, pp. 143–166.

72. *La Transcendance de l'Ego,* p. 89.

73. *Ibid.,* p. 90.

74. *Ibid.,* p. 96.

75. *Ibid.*

76. Varet, *L'ontologie de Sartre,* p. 101.

77. *L'Être et le Néant,* p. 115. Sartre belongs to the properly French tradition in his philosophy of consciousness, even though he opposes a Cartesian, Biranian, or Bergsonian conception of interiority. (Let us note, however, J. Beaufret's interpretation according to which the Dasein of Heidegger is consciousness through and through

inasmuch as it is *Erschlossenheit,* openness to the world. J. Beaufret, "A propos de l'existentialisme," *Confluences,* 1945, p. 310.)

78. Varet, *L'ontologie de Sartre,* p. 178.

79. "*Implizites Sich-selber-Wissen,*" in the expression of H. Schmalenbach, "Das Sein des Bewusstseins," *Philos. Anzeiger,* 1930, pp. 364–432.

80. *L'Être et le Néant,* p. 20. *La Transcendance de l'Ego,* p. 90.

81. *L'Être et le Néant,* p. 201.

82. *La Transcendance de l'Ego,* p. 90.

83. *L'Imaginaire,* p. 23.

84. *La Transcendance de l'Ego,* p. 91.

85. *L'Être et le Néant,* pp. 20, 22, 23.

86. When Heidegger reproaches Sartre on this point for having retained the classical or "metaphysical" sense of *existentia,* for limiting himself to reversing the traditional relationship between essence and existence, he is grossly mistaken (*Über den Humanismus,* p. 72). His polemic against Sartre betrays, moreover, the unhappy fact that he has not understood him.

87. "A propos de l'existentialisme," in the journal *Action,* reproduced in the review *Lettres* (Geneva), 1945, I, 82–88. *L'existentialisme est un humanisme,* 1946. Cf. Merleau-Ponty, *Sens et Non-Sens,* p. 96.

88. *La Nausée,* pp. 162–172.

89. *Lettres,* p. 86.

90. "*Visée du monde.*"

91. *La Transcendance de l'Ego,* p. 123.

92. *Situations,* II, 116.

93. *L'Être et le Néant,* p. 507, and *Situations,* II, 262.

94. *Situations,* III, 182.

95. *Ibid.,* pp. 182, 193. Already in Husserl the notion of constitutive *operation* or of creation (*Leistung*) took on an ever increasing importance. —The problem of action in the phenomenological perspective remains an open problem. See, on this subject, A. De Waelhens, "Vie intérieure et vie active," in *Les Droits de l'esprit et les exigences sociales* (Rencontres internationales de Genève), Neuchâtel, 1950, pp. 29–39, and the discussion, pp. 171–172.

96. *Situations,* III, 194.

97. *Situations,* I, 79.

98. *Ibid.* Note the reciprocal implication of the notion of nothingness and future in Sartre's conception of consciousness.

99. *L'Être et le Néant,* p. 169.

100. *Ibid.,* p. 520.

101. *Ibid.,* p. 188.

102. See above in Part I, pp. 52–53. Cf. *Problèmes actuels de la phénoménologie*, Paris, 1952, pp. 26–27.

103. *L'Être et le Néant*, p. 561; *Situations*, II, 86; *Saint Genet, comédien et martyr*, Paris, 1952, pp. 177 ff.

104. *Saint Genet*, p. 180.

105. *Ibid.*, p. 222.

106. *Ibid.*, p. 177.

107. *"Visée."*

108. As likewise for Bergson, *Les deux sources* . . . , pp. 268–270.

109. *L'existentialisme est un humanisme*, p. 95.

110. *Situations*, I, 153.

111. *L'Être et le Néant*, p. 654.

112. *Ibid.*, p. 288.

113. *Les Mouches*, p. 101; *Le Sursis*, pp. 166, 320.

114. *L'Être et le Néant*, p. 708.

115. We can only show here the culmination of Sartre's method; we cannot analyze his atheism as such. See on this subject: Pedro Descoqs, "L'athéisme de J.-P. Sartre" in *L'existentialisme*, Paris, 1949, pp. 39–89; H. Paissac, *Le Dieu de Sartre*, Paris, 1950. See also a critical exposition of the positions of Heidegger and Sartre in Karl Barth, *Kirchliche Dogmatik*, III/3, 1950, pp. 383–402.

116. *Le Diable et le Bon Dieu*, p. 252.

117. *Ibid.*, p. 235.

118. *Ibid.*, p. 267.

119. *Ibid.*, p. 269.

120. *Ibid.*, p. 275.

121. The whole question remains of knowing whether God is subject to such a reduction and if it is possible to manipulate God in the way the phenomenological reduction manipulates the world.

122. *Le Diable et le Bon Dieu*, p. 268.

123. As we see in *Situations* II and III, in *Les Mains Sales*, in *Le Diable et le Bon Dieu*, and most recently in the polemic between Camus and Sartre (*Temps Modernes*, August, 1952, pp. 317–353).

124. *Phénoménologie de la perception*, Avant-propos, p. i. Unless otherwise noted all the following citations are taken from this book.

125. *Ibid.*, pp. 231, 397, 418, 432, etc. One will find some particulars on ambiguity in the discussion of the Rencontres internationales de Genève, 1951, *La connaissance de l'homme au XXᵉ Siècle*, Neuchâtel, pp. 217–239.

126. *Ibid.*, pp. 469–520. A. De Waelhens, *Une philosophie de l'ambiguité*, p. 313, finds this criticism too severe. Concerning this book, see below.

127. Since the following exposition is terribly summary, good introductions to the philosophy of Merleau-Ponty can be found in the

following studies: Roland Caillois, "Note sur l'analyse réflexive et la réflexion phénoménologique," *Deucalion* I, Paris, 1946, pp. 127–139. *Id.*, "De la perception à l'histoire. La philosophie de M. Merleau-Ponty," *Deucalion* 2, 1947, pp. 59–85. *Id.*, "Destin de l'humanisme marxiste," *Critique*, March, 1948. *Id.*, "Le monde vécu et l'histoire," *L'homme, le monde et l'histoire*, Grenoble-Paris, 1948, pp. 85–110. F. Alquié, "Une philosophie de l'ambiguité, l'existentialisme de M. Merleau-Ponty," *Fontaine*, No. 59, April, 1947, pp. 47–70. F. Jeanson, *Le problème moral et la pensée de Sartre*, Paris, 1947, pp. 133–153, 302–311, and *passim*. M.-D. Philippe, "Exposé de la phénoménologie de M. Merleau-Ponty," *Nova et Vetera*, 1951, pp. 132–146. *Id.*, "Réflexions sur la phénoménologie de M. Merleau-Ponty," *ibid.*, pp. 198–209.

128. See the interesting elucidations of reduction in A. De Waelhens, *op. cit.*, pp. 89–93.

129. For any phenomenologist the world is understood on the basis of the fundamental structure of "being-in-the-world" and not vice versa.

130. *Phénoménologie de la perception*, p. 518; *Sens et Non-sens*, p. 72.

131. For a complete and detailed study of the philosophy of Merleau-Ponty, at once sympathetic and critical, we must refer the reader to the important and now indispensable work of Alphonse De Waelhens, *Une philosophie de l'ambiguité, l'existentialisme de Maurice Merleau-Ponty*, Louvain, 1951. At first sight it may seem strange that a large book should be devoted to the not very extensive work of a still young philosopher. But this is justified by the interest and originality of the thought of Merleau-Ponty on the one hand, and by the exceptional competence of the author on the other. De Waelhens does not restrict himself to giving a résumé or a paraphrase of Merleau-Ponty, but discusses his position point by point with constant references to Husserl, Heidegger, Sartre, etc. In this way we are not only introduced into a dense and difficult corpus, but also constantly enlightened by the best guide to the present-day problematic of phenomenology in general. Thanks to De Waelhens, we see better how the phenomenology of Merleau-Ponty brings us back unceasingly from the thing to the meaning, from being to existence, how the body and the soul (or consciousness) are involved with one another (every body is already significant and consciousness is always expressed in a body), and how the phenomenological notion of intentionality "proscribes" the idea of a "representative consciousness" (p. 90), the basis of all the traditional epistemologies. On this last point De Waelhens brings out with reason that the ambition of Mer-

leau-Ponty is analogous to that of Kant: "To make explicit the conditions underlying scientific experience" (p. 97). But while Kant reduces the world of experience to a "diversity" without unity, to a "fine spray of impressions," Merleau-Ponty educes an experience of the world that is global and originary, the existential and lived experience of perception, beyond psychologism and logic, beyond representative consciousness, or rather on this side of it. Note the import of the final discussion on the "principal difficulty" of this philosophy: "In what sense it is possible to render the possibility of writing a phenomenology of perception compatible with the thesis that it is impossible to get outside perception" (pp. 385 ff.).

132. *La Structure du comportement*, p. 271.

133. *La Structure du comportement*, p. 298; cf. *Phénoménologie de la perception*, p. 377.

134. *Phénoménologie de la perception*, p. xi.

135. *Ibid.*, p. 492.

136. *Ibid.*, pp. 342, 454.

137. *"Non-sens."*

138. "Le langage indirect et les voix du silence," *Temps modernes*, June, 1952, p. 2118.

139. *Sens et Non-sens*, p. 380.

140. Cf. *Phénoménologie de la perception*, pp. 203–232; *Sens et Non-sens*, pp. 15–49; "Sur la phénoménologie du langage," in *Problèmes actuels de la phénoménologie*, pp. 91–109; "Le langage indirect et les voix du silence," *Temps modernes*, June and July, 1952; and the announced volume *La prose du monde*. Cf. A. De Waelhens, *op. cit.*, pp. 150–165, 366–376.

141. *Phénoménologie de la perception*, p. 229.

142. Cf. *Humanisme et Terreur; Sens et Non-sens;* "L'homme et l'adversité," in *La connaissance de l'homme au XXᵉ siècle*, pp. 51–75; "Le langage indirect et les voix du silence," *Temps modernes*, July, 1952. Cf. A. De Waelhens, *op. cit.*, pp. 331–365 (with an interesting discussion of the theses of R. Aron and G. Lukacs).

143. *Sens et Non-sens*, p. 343.

144. *Ibid.*, p. 8.

145. *Ibid.*, p. 156.

146. *Humanisme et Terreur*, p. 12.

147. *Sens et Non-sens*, p. 157.

148. *Humanisme et Terreur*, p. 206.

149. *Ibid.*, p. xli.

150. *Ibid.*, p. 206.

151. *Sens et Non-sens*, p. 380.

152. *Phénoménologie de la perception*, p. 520.

THE QUESTION OF THE RADICAL POINT OF DEPARTURE IN DESCARTES AND HUSSERL

1. And not *archaeology* which is the science of antiquity. Husserl, who always regretted the fact that the word archaeology was already monopolized (E. Fink, "Das Problem der Phänomenologie E. Husserls," *Revue internationale de Philosophie*, 1938–39, I, 246), could well have availed himself of the neologism *archology*.

2. According to the expression of E. Pini (1803) and of V. Gioberti, *Della Protologia* (1857).

3. Aristotle, *Metaphysics*, 982 b 9.

4. "*Wissenschaft des Anfangs*," Husserl, *Nachwort zu meinen "Ideen*," p. 161.

5. Plato, *Theatetus*, 155 d, in the sense in which wonder is the source of philosophical reflexion.

6. "*Ein wirklicher Anfänger*," Husserl, *Nachwort zu meinen "Ideen*", p. 161.

7. See, for example, *Krisis*, pp. 11, 52, 77. That which is *Selbstverständlich* is at the same time *unverständlich*.

8. *Nachwort zu meinen "Ideen*", p. 147.

9. *Krisis*, pp. 11, 16.

10. Contrary to what Husserl imagines, "metaphysics" does not begin at the moment when Descartes, after having begun so well, weakens and falls back into the substantialist realism of the *res cogitans;* it begins already with the intervention of the evil genius (to which Husserl pays no attention at all).

11. *First Meditation*.

12. *Ibid*.

13. *Second Meditation*. [As always, the force and density of Descartes' expression is lost in English translation: "Je pense être, donc je suis."—Editor.]

14. In the *Discourse on Method*, in which the evil genius does not occur, the conclusion of the doubt is: I think, therefore I am. In the *Meditations*, precisely because of the *metaphysical* experience of the evil genius, it is simply: I am, I exist, or put differently: I think [myself] to be, therefore I am. ["Je pense être, donc je suis."]

15. *Verborgen, unbewusst; latent offenbar, wach*. Cf. *Krisis*, p. 13.

16. This attention is attention to self, since it is concentration and intensification. It manifests this movement of centripetal recollection which the prefix of *con*-sciousness indicates and to which the German term *Be-wusstsein* is not equivalent. In order to show clearly that this attention is not simply a psychological phenomenon, but an effort of concentration and of metaphysical apprehension of self, it would per-

haps be preferable (according to a suggestion which M. Philippe Devaux has kindly made to me and which I am taking up) to call it *contention*. [In French this word signifies primarily "prolonged effort," a meaning it has lost in English.—EDITOR.]

17. *Nachwort zu meinen "Ideen"*, p. 162.

18. *La philosophie comme prise de conscience de l'humanité*, *Deucalion* 3, p. 125.

19. *Krisis*, p. 59. Cf. *Logische Untersuchungen*, II, 17.

20. See *op. cit.*, in *Deucalion* 3, p. 125.

21. *Nachwort*, p. 161.

22. Cited by Walter Biemel in *Deucalion* 3, p. 113.

23. *Krisis*, pp. 72–73.

REFLEXION AND CONSCIOUSNESS OF SELF

1. Husserl, *Ideen*, p. 144 (trans. Ricoeur, p. 247). Cf. J.-P. Sartre, *L'Être et le Néant*, p. 197: "Toute notre ontologie [phénoménologique] a son fondement dans une expérience réflexive."

2. *Logische Untersuchungen*, II, 376.

3. *Ibid.*, p. 103.

4. *Ibid.*, p. 9; *Ideen*, p. 145 (trans. Ricoeur, p. 247).

5. *Ideen*, pp. 94–95 (trans. Ricoeur, pp. 166–167).

6. *Ibid.*, p. 145.

7. *La transcendance de l'Ego*.

8. In spite of the opinion of Husserl, who congratulated Descartes for having discovered "transcendental subjectivity," but who regretted that he compromised the transcendental meaning of his discovery by falling back into substantialist objectivism.

9. Cf. "What is Phenomenology?" above p. 70.

10. For, as concerns consciousness of objects, the superiority of Kantian or Husserlian transcendentalism over all the "naive" or pre-critical realisms (or idealisms) appears unquestionable.

GOING BEYOND METAPHYSICS

1. Letter to Markus Herz, 1871 (ed. Cassirer, IX, 198).

2. *Reflexionen Kants zur kritischen Philosophie*, ed. Erdmann, Leipzig, 1885, II, 50. However, there is no other going-beyond in philosophy than that, which like the Hegelian *Aufhebung*, abolishes by conserving. And Kant, as we know, by giving the coup de grâce to classical metaphysics, opened the door to contemporary metaphysics, relaunched philosophy on new paths, and prevented the decomposition already begun since Locke from becoming solidified by a relapse

pure and simple below the level of the metaphysical élan, in an a-philosophical or skeptical attitude à la Hume.

3. Jean Wahl, *Traité de Métaphysique*, Paris, 1953, p. 197.

4. According to the expression of Jean Wahl, *Existence humaine et transcendance, Être et Penser*, VI, 1944, pp. 37, 39.

5. *Republic*, 509 b–c.

6. *Enneads*, VI, 9, 6.

7. *De l'unité métaphysique*, p. 18.

8. Nicholas of Cusa, *Apologia*, ed. Klibansky, p. 12: "*sola docta ignorantia seu comprehensibilis incomprehensibilitatis.*"

9. In Pseudo-Denys we observe the influence of Christianity on metaphysics. The God who is incarnated and revealed in history, the *Logos* made flesh, troubled the élan by which the Greeks moved towards God and transcendence. For the first time it became necessary to lower oneself into the this-side in order to elevate oneself to God. The humiliation of Christ testifies to the rehabilitation of the sensible and of poverty, and certainly contributed in part to the conception of transcending metaphysics as a return to the this-side. What is more, if metaphysics is taxed with foolishness before God, the intellect is constrained to pose in all its acuteness the problem of its own foundation.

10. *Introduction à l'étude de saint Augustin*, p. 299.

11. *De vera religione*, 39, 72.

12. *De l'unité métaphysique*, pp. 94, 103.

13. *Revue internationale de philosophie*, II, 1939, p. 63.

14. *La philosophie* in *La Science française*, p. 16.

15. Only a Decoster or a Brunschvicg, influenced by Spinozist immanence, will refuse "*l'imagination en hauteur.*"

16. Later on Descartes will put human reason out of the reach of questioning by recurring to the divine guarantee; but that is another question.

17. The common notion of limit of knowledge, that of agnosticism, relativism, or skepticism, maintains on the contrary the reality of the beyond and remains faithful to traditional metaphysics. It simply judges that this metaphysical world is unknowable. Spencer is just the reverse of Kant.

18. See "What is Phenomenology?" in this volume.

19. Cf. Cornelio Fabro, *Ontologia esistenzialistica e metafisica tradizionale* in *La Metafisica classica*, Milan, 1954.

20. A. De Waelhens, *Chemins et impasses de l'ontologie heideggerienne*, Louvain, 1953, p. 27.

21. Heidegger, Prologue to the French translation of *Qu'est-ce que la Métaphysique?* p. 8.

22. J. Beaufret, *Martin Heidegger et le problème de la vérité,* *Fontaine,* November, 1947, p. 759.

23. *Kant und das Problem der Metaphysik,* Introduction and First Section.

24. *Ibid.,* p. 11; trans. by A. De Waelhens and W. Biemel, Paris, 1953, p. 72.

25. *Ibid.,* p. 205; trans. p. 272.

26. *Ibid.,* p. 195; trans. p. 261.

27. *Ibid.*

28. Max Müller, *Crise de la métaphysique,* 1953, p. 85.

29. *Kant und das Problem der Metaphysik,* p. 220; trans. p. 286.

30. *Vom Wesen der Wahrheit* (1943), *Über den Humanismus* (1947), Preface and Postface to the 6th ed. of *Was ist Metaphysik?* (1951), *Was heisst Denken?* (1952).

31. *Vom Wesen der Wahrheit,* p. 28; *Was ist Metaphysik?* p. 39, etc.

32. *Was ist Metaphysik?* p. 19.

33. *Ibid.,* p. 46.

34. Such is the final result even if Heidegger does assure us that he does not "think against metaphysics" and that metaphysics remains "what is primary in philosophy." But he adds that it does not attain in any case "what is primary in thinking" (*Was ist Metaphysik?* p. 9).

35. *Was ist Metaphysik?* p. 10.

36. *Ibid.,* p. 11.

37. *Ibid.,* p. 40.

38. *Ibid.*

39. *Über den Humanismus,* p. 119.

40. *Was ist Metaphysik?* p. 7.

41. *Ibid.,* p. 11.

42. Heidegger expresses his metaphysical revolution by saying that his question of 1930 was understood: Was ist *Metaphysik?* (How is it possible to found metaphysics?) whereas it ought to be understood: *Was* ist Metaphysik? which is to say: What is the reason for this unfortunate forgetting of Being which through the centuries is characteristic of metaphysics? (p. 39).

43. "To interpret by beginning at the end." *Was ist Metaphysik?* p. 21.

44. Despite all that radically separates him from the positivists (cf. Max Müller, *Crise de la Métaphysique,* p. 86).

45. As the book by Egon Vietta, *Die Seinsfrage bei Heidegger,* Stuttgart, 1950, attests. [Commenting on this book by Egon Vietta in another connection (*Revue de Théologie et de Philosophie,* 1952, p. 140) Thévenaz writes: "One finds in this book a dithyrambic admiration for the master, the friend of wisdom, the robust recluse of

the Black Forest, whose theory of truth is the most audacious dramaturgy of human history, and therefore of man, which has ever been thought. One feels a certain uneasiness in the atmosphere of this philosophical chapel which is a little too conscious of being the *Da* where the *Sein* has deigned to manifest itself."—EDITOR.]

46. Louis Lavelle, "La métaphysique ou la science de l'intimité spirituelle," *Revue internationale de philosophie*, II, 1939, p. 48.

47. Kant, Letter to Markus Herz.

48. Jean Hyppolite with reference to Heidegger's "Que signifie penser?" in *Mercure de France*, March, 1953, p. 387.

49. Merleau-Ponty, *Phénoménologie de la perception*, p. 419.

50. Jean Wahl, *Traité de Métaphysique*, p. 689.

BIBLIOGRAPHY

[In his essay "What is Phenomenology?" Pierre Thévenaz included several excellent bibliographical sections. However, since these are now somewhat out of date and since they were directed to French readers, they have been omitted from this translation. In their place the following bibliography was composed for the use of students and those seeking trustworthy introductions to the thought of the four principal phenomenologists who appear in these pages. This bibliography lists the principal works of these authors and all translations available in English at the present time. It also includes a restricted list of major studies (no articles or periodical literature) in English on Husserl, Heidegger, and Sartre; there are no important publications on Merleau-Ponty in the English language.

Since the *philosophical* literature on phenomenology and existentialism in the English language is of surprisingly poor quality, it has not been felt necessary to list all the titles that exist on these authors. Instead, the list has been restricted to those books which can be clearly recommended because of their value as serious introductions to the philosophical thought of the authors concerned, without thereby passing judgment on any titles not included.

Moreover, the reader will find a very useful introduction to the whole field of phenomenology in Herbert Spiegelberg, *The Phenomenological Movement, A Historical Introduction,* 2 vols. Nijhoff, The Hague, 1960. These volumes contain extensive bibliographies on all aspects of phenomenology, including articles that have appeared in journals and reviews.—Editor.]

EDMUND HUSSERL

Major Works:

Philosophie der Arithmetik, Vol. I, Halle: Pfeffer, 1891.

185

Logische Untersuchungen, Vol. I (1900), Vol. II (1901); second revised edition in 3 vols., Halle: Niemeyer, 1913.

"Philosophie als strenge Wissenschaft," *Logos,* I (1910), 289-314.

——Translation by Quentin Lauer, "Philosophy as a Strict Science," in Edmund Husserl, *Phenomenology and the Crisis of Reason,* New York: Harper, 1965, pp. 71-147.

Ideen zu einer reinen Phänomenologie und phänomenologischen Philosophie, Vol. I, Halle: Niemeyer, 1913; a new edition of Vol. I and Vols. II and III comprise *Husserliana* III-V (1950–1952).[1]

——Translation of Vol. I by W. R. Boyce Gibson, *Ideas: General Introduction to Pure Phenomenology,* New York: Macmillan, 1931.

——A summary of *Ideen* II and III is given by Alfred Schuetz in *Philosophy and Phenomenological Research,* XIII (1953), 394–413, 506–514.

"Phenomenology," an article in *Encyclopaedia Britannica,* 14th ed., 1927, Vol. 17, 699–702.

Vorlesungen zur Phänomenologie des inneren Zeitbewusstseins, Halle: Niemeyer, 1928.[2]

——Translation by James S. Churchill, *The Phenomenology of Internal Time-Consciousness,* Bloomington: Indiana University Press, 1964.

Formale und transzendentale Logik, Halle: Niemeyer, 1929.

Nachwort zu meinen Ideen zu einer reinen Phänomenologie, Halle: Niemeyer, 1930.

Méditations cartésiennes, Paris: A. Colin, 1931; republished by Vrin, Paris, 1947; also *Cartesianische Meditationen und Pariser Vorträge* in *Husserliana* I (1950).

——Translation by Dorian Cairns, *Cartesian Meditations,* The Hague: Nijhoff, 1960.

——Translation by Peter Koestenbaum, *The Paris Lectures,* The Hague: Nijhoff, 1964.

Die Krisis der europäischen Wissenschaften und die transzendentale Phänomenologie, Part I, *Philosophia,* 1936; all extant parts are published in *Husserliana* VI (1954).

——A summary by Aron Gurwitsch in *Philosophy and Phenomenological Research,* XVI (1956), 380–399, and XVII (1957), 370–398.

——Translation of "Philosophy and Crisis of European Man," a

1. The complete works of Husserl being published at The Hague by Nijhoff.

2. This and other important phenomenological works first appeared in Husserl's journal: *Jahrbuch für philosophie und phänomenologische forschung,* 11 vols., Halle: Niemeyer, 1916-1930.

lecture given at the University of Prague in May, 1935, by Quentin Lauer, in Edmund Husserl, *Phenomenology and the Crisis of Philosophy*, New York: Harper, 1965, pp. 149-192.

Erfahrung und Urteil, Untersuchungen zur Genealogie der Logik, published posthumously by Ludwig Landgrebe, Academia-Verlag, Prague, 1939, republished by Classen & Goverts, Hamburg, 1948.

Die Idee der Phänomenologie, Fünf Vorlesungen (1907), published posthumously in *Husserliana* II (1958).

——Translation by William P. Alston and George Nakhnikian, *The Idea of Phenomenology*, The Hague: Nijhoff, 1964.

Erste Philosophie (1923–1924), published posthumously in *Husserliana* VII and VIII (1956–1959).

STUDIES IN ENGLISH:

Marvin Farber, *The Foundation of Phenomenology, Edmund Husserl and the Quest for a Rigorous Science of Philosophy*, Cambridge: Harvard University Press, 1943.

Marvin Farber, ed., *Philosophical Essays in Memory of Edmund Husserl*, Cambridge: Harvard University Press, 1940.

Quentin Lauer, S.J., *The Triumph of Subjectivity, An Introduction to Transcendental Phenomenology*, New York: Fordham University Press, 1958.

Aron Gurwitsch, *The Field of Consciousness*, Pittsburgh: Duquesne University Press, 1964.

MARTIN HEIDEGGER

MAJOR WORKS:

Die Kategorien-und Bedeutungslehre des Duns Scotus, Tübingen: Mohr, 1916.

Sein und Zeit, Halle: Niemeyer, 1927.

——Translation by John Macquarrie and Edward Robinson, *Being and Time*, Oxford: Blackwell's, 1962.

"Vom Wesen des Grundes," in *Festschrift für E. Husserl*, Halle: Niemeyer, 1929; also published separately by Klostermann, Frankfurt, 1949.

Kant und das Problem der Metaphysik, Bonn: Cohen, 1929.

——Translation by James S. Churchill, *Kant and the Problem of Metaphysics*, Bloomington: Indiana University Press, 1962.

Was ist Metaphysik? Frankfurt: Klostermann, 1929; "Nachwort" (1944); "Einleitung" (1951).

——Translation by R. F. C. Hull and Alan Crick, "What Is Metaphysics?" in *Existence and Being*, Werner Brock, ed., Chicago: Regnery, 1949.

——Translation of the "Einleitung" by Walter Kaufmann, "The Way Back into the Ground of Metaphysics," in *Existentialism from Dostoevsky to Sartre*, New York: Meridian, 1956, pp. 207–221.

Die Selbstbehauptung der deutschen Universität, Breslau: Korn, 1934.

Hölderlin und das Wesen der Dichtung, Pfullingen: Neske, 1936.

——Translation by Douglas Scott, "Hölderlin and the Essence of Poetry," in *Existence and Being*.

Vom Wesen der Wahreit, Frankfurt: Klostermann, 1943.

——Translation by R. F. C. Hull and Alan Crick, "On the Essence of Truth," in *Existence and Being*.

Platons Lehre von der Wahrheit with "Brief über den Humanismus," Berne: Francke, 1947.

——Translation by John Barlow and Edgar Lohner for *Philosophy in the Twentieth Century*, ed. William Barrett and Henry D. Aiken, New York: Random House, 1962, II, 251-302.

Holzwege, Frankfurt: Klostermann, 1950.

——Translation of the second essay by Marjorie Grene, "The Age of the World View," in *Measure* (1951), pp. 269–284.

Einführung in die Metaphysik, Tübingen: Niemeyer, 1953.

——Translation by Ralph Manheim, *An Introduction to Metaphysics*, New Haven: Yale University Press, 1959.

Was heisst Denken? Tübingen: Niemeyer, 1954.

Aus der Erfahrung des Denkens, Pfullingen: Neske, 1954.

Vorträge und Aufsätze, Pfullingen: Neske, 1954.

Was ist das-die Philosophie? Pfullingen: Neske, 1956.

——Translation by W. Kluback and Jean T. Wilde, *What Is Philosophy?* London: Vision, 1958.

Der Satz vom Grund, Pfullingen: Neske, 1958.

Identität und Differenz, Pfullingen: Neske, 1957.

——Translation by Kurt F. Leidecker, *Essays in Metaphysics: Identity and Difference*, New York: Philosophical Library, 1960.

Unterwegs zur sprache, Pfullingen: Neske, 1960.

Nietzsche, 2 vols., Pfullingen: Neske, 1961.

STUDIES IN ENGLISH:

The following books have helpful expository sections on Heidegger.

William Barrett, *Irrational Man*, New York: Doubleday, 1958.

John Macquarrie, *An Existentialist Theology; a comparison of Heidegger and Bultmann*, London: SCM Press, 1955.

Kurt Reinhardt, *The Existentialist Revolt*, Milwaukee: Bruce, 1952.

Calvin O. Schrag, *Existence and Freedom*, Evanston: Northwestern University Press, 1961.

John D. Wild, *The Challenge of Existentialism*, Bloomington: Indiana University Press, 1955.

JEAN-PAUL SARTRE

MAJOR WORKS:

L'Imagination, Paris: Alcan; also Paris: Presses Universitaires de France, 1948.

——Translation by Forrest Williams, *Imagination*, Ann Arbor: The University of Michigan Press, 1962.

"La Transcendance de l'égo," *Recherches philosophiques*, VI (1936), 85–123.

——Translation by Forrest Williams and Robert Kirkpatrick, *The Transcendence of the Ego*, New York: Noonday, 1957.

La Nausée, Paris: Gallimard, 1938.

——Translation by Lloyd Alexander, *Nausea*, Norfolk, Connecticut: New Directions, 1949.

Esquisse d'une théorie des émotions, Paris: Hermann, 1939.

——Translation by B. Frechtman, *The Emotions: Outline of a Theory*, New York: Philosophical Library, 1948.

L'Imaginaire: Psychologie-phénoménologique de l'imagination, Paris: Gallimard, 1940.

——Anonymous translation, *Psychology of Imagination*, New York: Philosophical Library, 1948.

Les Mouches, Paris: Gallimard, 1943.

——Translation by Stuart Gilbert, "The Flies," in *No Exit, and Three Other Plays*, New York: Vintage Books, 1955.

Huis Clos, Paris: Gallimard, 1943.

——Translation by Stuart Gilbert, *No Exit, and Three Other Plays*. Also in this volume are *Dirty Hands (Les mains sales)* and *The Respectful Prostitute (La putain respectueuse)*, translated by Lionel Abel.

L'Être et le néant, Essai d'ontologie phénoménologique, Paris: Gallimard, 1943.

——Translation by Hazel Barnes, *Being and Nothingness, an Essay on Phenomenological Ontology*, New York: Philosophical Library, 1956.

L'âge de raison, Paris: Gallimard, 1945.

——Translation by Eric Sutton, *The Age of Reason*, New York: Knopf, 1947.

Le sursis, Paris: Gallimard, 1945.

——Translation by Eric Sutton, *The Reprieve*, New York: Knopf, 1947.

L'Existentialisme est un humanisme, Paris: Nagel, 1946.

——Translation by Philip Mairet, *Existentialism and Humanism*, London: Methuen, 1949. This translation also appears in Walter Kaufmann, ed., *Existentialism from Dostoevsky to Sartre*, New York: Meridian, 1956. Another translation is by B. Frechtman, *Existentialism*, New York: Philosophical Library, 1947.

Réflexions sur la question juive, Paris: Morihien, 1946.

——Translation by George J. Baker, *Anti-Semite and Jew*, New York: Schocken, 1948. Another translation by Mary Guggenheim appeared in *Partisan Review* (Spring, 1946), and also as "Portrait of the Anti-Semite," in *Existentialism from Dostoevsky to Sartre*.

"Forgers of Myths, the Young Playwrights of France," *Theatre Arts*, XXX (1946), 324–335.

Baudelaire, Paris: Gallimard, 1947.

——Translation by Martin Turnell, *Baudelaire*, Norfolk, Connecticut: New Directions, 1950.

Situations, 6 *vols.*, Paris: Gallimard, 1947, 1948, 1949, 1964, 1965.

——Translation of parts of Vols. I and III, by Anette Michelson, *Literary and Philosophical Essays*, New York: Criterion Books, 1955.

——Translation of part of Vol. II by B. Frechtman, *What Is Literature?* New York: Philosophical Library, 1949.

Visages, précédé de Portraits officiels, Paris: Seghers, 1948.

La mort dans l'âme, Paris: Gallimard, 1949.

——Translation by Gerard Hopkins, *Troubled Sleep*, New York: Knopf, 1951.

Le Diable et le bon Dieu, Paris: Gallimard, 1951.

——Translation by Kitty Black, *The Devil and the Good Lord*, New York: Knopf, 1960.

Saint Genet, comédien et martyr, Paris: Gallimard, 1952.

——Translation by Bernard Frechtman, *Saint Genet, Actor and Martyr*, New York: Braziller, 1963.

"Questions de méthode," *Les Temps Modernes*, XIII (1957), 338–417, 658–697.

Critique de la raison dialectique, précédé de Question de méthode, tome I, Paris: Gallimard, 1960.

——Translation of the "Introduction" by Hazel Barnes, *A Search for a Method*, New York: Knopf, 1963.

Essays in Aesthetics, selected and translated by Wade Baskin, New York: Philosophical Library, 1963.

Les Mots, Paris: Gallimard, 1964.
——Translation by Bernard Frechtman, *The Words,* New York: Braziller, 1964.

STUDIES IN ENGLISH:

Maurice Natanson, *A Critique of Jean-Paul Sartre's Ontology,* Lincoln, Nebraska: The University Press, 1951.
The following books have helpful expository sections on Sartre.
William Barrett, *Irrational Man,* New York: Doubleday, 1958.
H. J. Blackham, *Six Existentialist Thinkers,* New York: Harper Torchbooks, 1959.
Kurt Reinhardt, *The Existentialist Revolt,* Milwaukee: Bruce, 1952.

MAURICE MERLEAU-PONTY

MAJOR WORKS:

La Structure du comportement (1942), 2nd ed., revised and augmented, Paris: Presses universitaires de France, 1949.
——Translation by Alden L. Fisher, *The Structure of Behavior,* Boston: Beacon Press, 1963.
Phénoménologie de la perception, Paris: Gallimard, 1945.
——Translation by Colin Smith, *Phenomenology of Perception,* London: Routledge & Kegan Paul, and New York: Humanities Press, 1962.
Humanisme et terreur, Paris: Gallimard, 1947.
Sens et non-sens, Paris: Nagel, 1948.
——Translation by Hubert L. Dreyfus and Patricia Allen Dreyfus, *Sense and Non-Sense,* Evanston: Northwestern University Press, 1964.
Éloge de la philosophie, Paris: Gallimard, 1953.
——Translation by John Wild and James M. Edie, *In Praise of Philosophy,* Evanston: Northwestern University Press, 1963.
Les aventures de la dialectique, Paris: Gallimard, 1955.
Signes, Paris: Gallimard, 1960.
——Translation by Richard C. McCleary, *Signs,* Evanston: Northwestern University Press, 1964.
The Primacy of Perception and Other Essays, edited by James M. Edie, Evanston: Northwestern University Press, 1964.
Le visible et l'invisible, Paris: Gallimard, 1965.

QUADRANGLE PAPERBACKS

American History

Frederick Lewis Allen.
The Lords of Creation. (QP35)
Lewis Atherton.
Main Street on the Middle Border. (QP36)
Thomas A. Bailey.
Woodrow Wilson and the Lost Peace. (QP1)
Thomas A. Bailey. *Woodrow Wilson and the Great Betrayal.* (QP2)
Charles A. Beard.
The Idea of National Interest. (QP27)
Carl L. Becker.
Everyman His Own Historian. (QP33)
Ray A. Billington.
The Protestant Crusade. (QP12)
Allan G. Bogue.
From Prairie to Corn Belt. (QP50)
Kenneth E. Boulding.
The Organizational Revolution. (QP43)
David M. Chalmers.
Hooded Americanism. (QP51)
John Chamberlain.
Farewell to Reform. (QP19)
Alice Hamilton Cromie.
A Tour Guide to the Civil War.
Robert D. Cross. *The Emergence of Liberal Catholicism in America.* (QP44)
Chester McArthur Destler.
American Radicalism, 1865-1901. (QP30)
Robert A. Divine.
The Illusion of Neutrality. (QP45)
Elisha P. Douglass.
Rebels and Democrats. (QP26)
Herman Finer. *Road to Reaction.* (QP5)
Felix Frankfurter.
The Commerce Clause. (QP16)
Lloyd C. Gardner.
A Different Frontier. (QP32)
Edwin Scott Gaustad. *The Great Awakening in New England.* (QP46)
Ray Ginger. *Altgeld's America.* (QP21)
Louis Hartz. *Economic Policy and Democratic Thought.* (QP52)
William B. Hesseltine.
Lincoln's Plan of Reconstruction. (QP41)
Dwight W. Hoover.
Understanding Negro History. (QP49)
Stanley P. Hirshson.
Farewell to the Bloody Shirt. (QP53)
Frederic C. Howe.
The Confessions of a Reformer. (QP39)
Louis Joughin and Edmund M. Morgan.
The Legacy of Sacco and Vanzetti. (QP7)
William Loren Katz. *Teachers' Guide to American Negro History.* (QP210)
Edward Chase Kirkland. *Dream and Thought in the Business Community, 1860-1900.* (QP11)
Edward Chase Kirkland.
Industry Comes of Age. (QP42)
Adrienne Koch.
The Philosophy of Thomas Jefferson. (QP17)
Gabriel Kolko.
The Triumph of Conservatism. (QP40)
Walter LaFeber. *John Quincy Adams and American Continental Empire.* (QP23)
David E. Lilienthal.
TVA: Democracy on the March. (QP28)
Arthur S. Link.
Wilson the Diplomatist. (QP18)
Huey P. Long. *Every Man a King.* (QP8)
Gene M. Lyons.
America: Purpose and Power. (QP24)
Jackson Turner Main.
The Antifederalists. (QP14)
Ernest R. May. *The World War and American Isolation, 1914-1917.* (QP29)
Henry F. May.
The End of American Innocence. (QP9)

George E. Mowry.
The California Progressives. (QP6)
Frank L. Owsley.
Plain Folk of the Old South. (QP22)
David Graham Phillips.
The Treason of the Senate. (QP20)
Julius W. Pratt.
Expansionists of 1898. (QP15)
Moses Rischin.
The American Gospel of Success. (QP54)
John P. Roche.
The Quest for the Dream. (QP47)
David A. Shannon.
The Socialist Party of America. (QP38)
John Spargo.
The Bitter Cry of the Children. (QP55)
Richard W. Van Alstyne.
The Rising American Empire. (QP25)
Willard M. Wallace.
Appeal to Arms. (QP10)
Norman Ware.
The Industrial Worker, 1840-1860. (QP13)
Albert K. Weinberg. *Manifest Destiny.* (QP3)
Bernard A. Weisberger.
They Gathered at the River. (QP37)
Robert H. Wiebe.
Businessmen and Reform. (QP56)
Bell I. Wiley. *The Plain People of the Confederacy.* (QP4)
William Appleman Williams.
The Contours of American History. (QP34)
William Appleman Williams.
The Great Evasion. (QP48)
Esmond Wright. *Causes and Consequences of the American Revolution.* (QP31)

European History

William Sheridan Allen.
The Nazi Seizure of Power. (QP302)
W. O. Henderson. *The Industrial Revolution in Europe.* (QP303)
Raul Hilberg. *The Destruction of the European Jews.* (QP301)

Philosophy

F. H. Bradley. *The Presuppositions of Critical History.* (QP108)
William Earle. *Objectivity.* (QP109)
James M. Edie.
An Invitation to Phenomenology. (QP103)
James M. Edie.
Phenomenology in America. (QP105)
Manfred S. Frings.
Heidegger and the Quest for Truth. (QP107)
Moltke S. Gram.
Kant: Disputed Questions. (QP104)
George L. Kline.
European Philosophy Today. (QP102)
Lionel Rubinoff.
Faith and Reason. (QP106)
Pierre Thévenaz.
What Is Phenomenology? (QP101)

Political Science

Charles O. Lerche, Jr.
Last Chance in Europe. (QP207)
David Mitrany.
A Working Peace System. (QP205)

Social Science

George and Eunice Grier.
Equality and Beyond. (QP204)
Martin Oppenheimer and George Lakey.
A Manual for Direct Action. (QP202)
Fred Powledge. *To Change a Child.* (QP209)
Lee Rainwater.
And the Poor Get Children. (QP208)
Clarence Senior. *The Puerto Ricans.* (QP201)